What Hedge Funds Really Do

What Hedge Funds Really Do

An Introduction to Portfolio Management

Philip J. Romero and Tucker Balch

BEP BUSINESS EXPERT PRESS

What Hedge Funds Really Do: An Introduction to Portfolio Management
Copyright © Business Expert Press, LLC, 2014.

First published in 2014 by
Business Expert Press, LLC
222 East 46th Street, New York, NY 10017
www.businessexpertpress.com

ISBN-13: 9781953349064
ISBN-13: 978-1-63157-090-2 (e-book)

Business Expert Press Economics Collection

Collection ISSN: 2163-761X (print)
Collection ISSN: 2163-7628 (electronic)

Cover and interior design by Exeter Premedia Services Private Ltd.,
Chennai, India

First edition: 2014

10 9 8 7 6 5 4 3 2 1

Abstract

What do hedge funds really do? These lightly regulated funds continually innovate new investing and trading strategies to take advantage of temporary mispricing of assets (when their market price deviates from their intrinsic value). These techniques are shrouded in mystery, which permits hedge fund managers to charge exceptionally high fees. While the details of each fund's approach are carefully guarded trade secrets, this book draws the curtain back on the core building blocks of many hedge fund strategies. As an instructional text, it will assist two types of students:

- Economics and finance students interested in understanding what "quants" do, and
- Software specialists interested in applying their skills to programming trading systems.

What Hedge Funds Really Do provides a needed complement to journalistic accounts of the hedge fund industry, to deepen the understanding of nonspecialist readers such as policy makers, journalists, and individual investors. The book is organized in modules to allow different readers to focus on the elements of this topic that most interest them. Its authors include a fund practitioner and a computer scientist (Balch), in collaboration with a public policy economist and finance academic (Romero).

Keywords

absolute return, active investment management, arbitrage, capital asset pricing model, CAPM, derivatives, exchange traded funds, ETF, fat tails, finance, hedge funds, hedging, high-frequency trading, HFT, investing, investment management, long/short, modern portfolio theory, MPT, optimization, quant, quantitative trading strategies, portfolio construction, portfolio management, portfolio optimization, trading, trading strategies, Wall Street

Contents

PART I
The Basics

CHAPTER 1

Introduction

George Soros, a poor Hungarian immigrant with a philosopher's bent and a London School of Economics degree, founded Quantum Capital in the late 1960s and led it to breathtaking returns, famously "breaking the Bank of England" in 1992 by shorting the pound sterling. Julian Robertson, the hard-charging North Carolina charmer who made huge contrarian bets on stocks, built the Tiger Fund in the 1970s and seeded dozens of Tiger Cubs that collectively manage hundreds of billions of dollars. John Meriwether left Salomon Brothers to collect a stable of PhDs in quantitative finance from University of Chicago to form the envied, and later notorious, Long Term Capital Management (LTCM). Each of these groups earned persistent returns for their investors that exceeded 30 percent per year, handily trouncing the market indexes. Each of their partners became billionaires, likely faster than ever before in history.

Each of these financial legends, and hundreds of other lesser-known investors, built a *hedge fund*. Private pools of funds have existed for as long as liquid capital markets—at least 800 years—but the first hedge fund is generally thought to be Albert Winslow Jones' "hedged fund," formed in the late 1940s. Since then, the number of such funds has grown into the thousands, and they manage trillions of dollars in clients' funds.

Hedge funds are the least understood form of Wall Street institution—partly by design. They are secretive, clannish, and less visible. Hedge funds have received a generous share of envy when they are successful and demonization when financial markets have melted down. But whether you wish to join them or beat them, first you need to understand them, and how they make their money.

Hedge funds are pools of money from "accredited" investors—relatively wealthy individuals and institutions assumed to have sufficient sophistication to protect their own interests. Therefore, unlike publicly

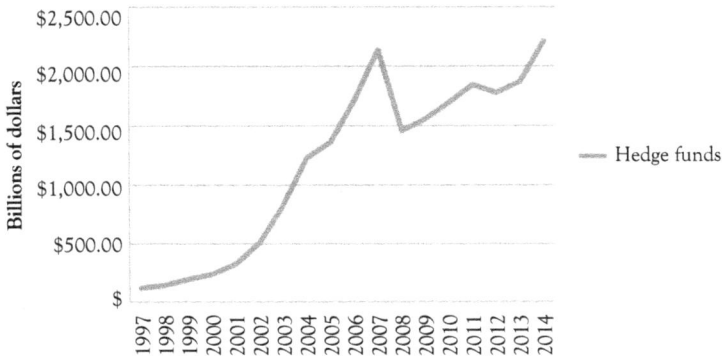

Figure 1.1 Total hedge fund assets under management, 1997 to 2013

traded company stock, mutual funds, and exchange traded funds (ETFs), hedge funds are exempt from most of the laws governing institutions that invest on behalf of clients. Implicitly, policy makers seem to believe that little regulation is necessary. The absence of scrutiny has helped hedge funds keep their trading strategies secret.

The scale of hedge funds has grown tremendously in the past few decades, as illustrated in Figure 1.1. The amount of funds under management has grown by a factor of 15 from 1997 to 2013. Hedge funds today represent a large minority of all liquid assets in the United States, and only a somewhat smaller fraction worldwide (Figure 1.2).

These lightly regulated funds continually adopt innovative investing and trading strategies to take advantage of temporary mispricing of assets (when their market price deviates from their intrinsic value). These techniques are shrouded in mystery, which permits hedge fund managers to charge exceptionally high fees. While the details of the approach of each of the funds are carefully guarded trade secrets, this book draws the curtain back on the core building blocks of many hedge fund strategies. As an instructional text, it will assist two types of students:

- Economics and finance students interested in understanding what "quants" do, and
- Software specialists interested in applying their skills to programming trading systems.

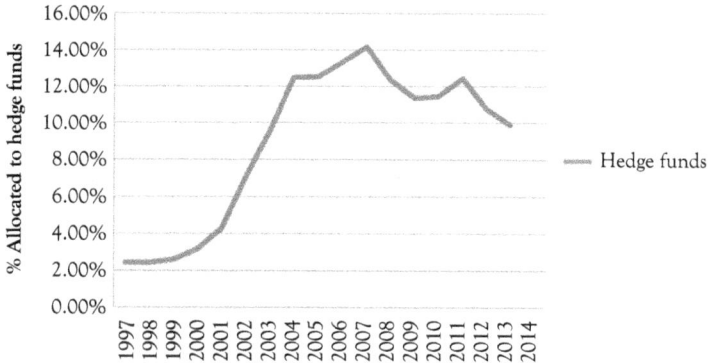

Figure 1.2 Hedge funds compared with other asset classes

A number of fine journalistic accounts of the industry exist—and should be read by anyone interested in understanding this industry—which offer interesting character studies and valuable cautionary tales. These include *The Quants* by Scott Patterson (2010), *The Big Short* and *Flash Boys* by Michael Lewis (2010 and 2014, respectively), *More Money Than God: Hedge Funds and The Making of the New Elite* by Sebastian Mallaby (2010), and *When Genius Failed: The Rise and Fall of Long-Term Capital Management* (2000) by Roger Lowenstein. But none dives very deeply into *how* quantitative strategies work. Many readers seek such tools so that they can improve current practice—from the inside, at hedge funds; or from the outside, as regulators, journalists, or advocates.

This book is a modest attempt to explain what hedge funds really do. Our focus is on the trading strategies that hedge funds use. We will provide basic investing and portfolio management background to the uninitiated, then move on to the computational details of efforts to automate trading strategies in machine learning systems.

This book is organized in modules; not all modules will be of interest to all readers. The main elements are as follows:

- Part I (*Investing Basics*) is a short introduction to investing for readers without prior financial training. Those with such training will find it worth a scan to refresh your recollection.

- Part II (*Investing Fundamentals*) outlines how to "optimize" a collection of investments—a portfolio—to maximize the ratio of return to risk within any constraints imposed by your situation.
- Parts I and II together constitute the financial background that computer scientists will need to program trading systems. Part III constitutes the core techniques of interest to programmers.
- Part III (*Market Simulation and Portfolio Construction*) describes the heart of most "quant" (quantitative) hedge funds' strategies—testing proposed trading rules based on historical market experience.
- Part IV (*Case Study and Future Directions*) provides important context regarding recent and prospective developments in the hedge fund industry, which will set the environment in which investors and programmers will operate.
- Finally, the back matter includes a glossary and a list of related teaching cases for use by instructors who use this book in their courses.

The book will be of interest to a variety of readers:

- Individual investors considering investing in "quant" mutual funds and ETFs, which are increasingly prevalent as Wall Street Markets "absolute return" and "liquid alternative" products to you.
- IT students who need to understand the investing background behind the trading systems they will design and program.
- Finance students who need an introduction to the IT underlying trading systems.
- Investing students who wish to understand how quant strategies can affect their portfolios.
- Public policy makers interested in asset market regulation.
- Journalists who wish to understand the markets they cover.

Read carefully the portions least familiar to you, and skim the familiar parts for refresher.

The two authors are, respectively, an economist and a former government official who made public policy regarding financial institutions; and a robotics specialist and former fighter pilot who founded a software firm that designs analytic platforms for hedge funds. We bring diverse perspectives to this topic, and we imagine that you may likewise be interested in more than one aspect. This book is broader than it is deep. We hope we stimulate your appetite to learn more about this growing, powerful, but little-known industry—and about the techniques that built its power.

Bio: Julian Robertson, Tiger Management

Born: Julian Harr Robertson, 1932

Firm: Tiger Management

Operated: 1980 to 2000 (seeded "Tiger Seeds" and "Tiger Cubs" in the early 2000s)

Annual return: 31.7 percent (1980 to 1998); 26 percent (1980 to 2000)

AUM at peak: $22 billion (1998)

Style: Long/short equity; added an international macro overlay in the 1990s

Robertson background: Raised in North Carolina, with a syrupy Southern charm. During the 1970s when working at Kidder Peabody, Robertson befriended Bob Burch, A. W. Jones's son-in-law, and later Jones himself. Robertson quizzed Jones about trading strategies and hedge fund structures.

When he formed Tiger in 1980, Burch invested $ 5 million, 20 percent of the surviving Jones assets.

Differentiation: Tiger emphasized bottom-up domestic stock selection, adding international equities and a global macro view in the early 1990s. "Our mandate is to find the 200 best companies in the world and invest in them, and find the 200 worst companies in the world and go short on them. If the 200 best don't do better than the 200 worst, you should probably be in another business."

Color: "Tall, confident, and athletic of build, he was a guy's guy, a jock's jock, and he hired in his own image. To thrive at Tiger Management, you almost needed the physique: otherwise, you would be hard-pressed to survive the Tiger retreats, which involved vertical hikes and outward-bound contests....The Tigers would fly out west…and be taken to a hilltop. They would split up into teams, each equipped with logs the size of telephone poles, some rope, and two paddles. They would heave the equipment down to the nearby lake, lash the logs together, and race out to a buoy—with the twist that not all of the team could fit on the raft, so some had to plunge into the icy water" (from Mallaby's More Money Than God).

Legacy: After Robertson restructured and wound down Tiger in 1998 to 2000, he seeded 36 funds founded by Tiger alumni, deemed "Tiger Seeds" and "Tiger Cubs." According to Hennessee group LLC hedge fund advisory, the 18 Tiger Cubs for which performance information could be found returned nearly three times Hennessee's index of long/short hedge funds (11.89 percent vs. 4.44 percent annually) from 2000 to 2008, with slightly less risk (7.42 percent vs. 7.76 percent standard deviation), yielding nearly 3 times the Sharpe ratio (1.42 for the cubs vs. 0.47 for the index). Robertson's personal investments in Tiger offspring perform handsomely: Forbes *reports that in 2009 his personal trading account earned 150 percent.*

CHAPTER 2

So You Want to Be a Hedge Fund Manager

You are reading this book because of your interest in hedge funds: you want to work in one, maybe establish a new one; or you want to regulate them, write about them, perhaps even abolish them. In any case, you need to understand what they are and how they do what they do.

In this book we strive to present the essential concepts for quantitative fund management. We need to make some assumptions about our audience in order to frame our presentation. So we will assume you want to manage a fund, and we'll get you started on the basics from that viewpoint. We will also focus on stocks in the U.S. markets.

Let's first start with some context. What is *investing*, and how does that relate to *stocks*?

The Economic Role of Investing

Economies grow by applying accumulated capital, along with other resources, to produce increasing amounts of goods and services. Capital is accumulated from the savings of households when they do not consume all of their income. Savings are invested in financial instruments if they can offer an attractive return. So available capital is constrained by household savings, and the investments that households make will be those expected to have the best prospects (to offer the best prospective return). Those finite resources (savings) are used most efficiently if there are institutions that help redeploy capital from assets with a poor return to those with superior return. That is the role for the financial sector, of which hedge funds are a major part.

Investors can deploy their savings to a variety of financial instruments and institutions. The simplest version is to buy specific instruments, like *individual stocks and bonds.* The problem for small investors is that they may not have enough capital to diversify over a range of instruments to control risk. *Mutual funds* pool several investors' capital together and collectively purchase a diverse portfolio consistent with the fund's charter (e.g., large and mature companies; or small, speculative companies; or short-term corporate bonds; or long-term municipal bonds). "Mutual funds" are their American name; they go by other names elsewhere, such as unit investment trusts in the United Kingdom. Mutual funds allow small investors to achieve diversification. As such, they are heavily regulated—by the Securities and Exchange Commission (SEC) under the Investment Company Act of 1940 in the United States, for instance.

What Are Hedge Funds?

Mutual funds are restricted to investing pursuant to their charter, outlined to prospective investors in a "prospectus." Most funds aspire to be fully invested most of the time. The first hedge fund, created by ex-journalist Albert Winslow Jones in 1949, specifically undertook a more flexible investing style. Jones specifically would "pair" trades, for instance, identifying two companies whose fortunes he expected to move in opposite directions—say two competitors in a duopolistic industry. Jones would buy stock in one company ("go long" that company) and bet against the competitor ("go short" the competitor). This was a "hedged" strategy, in that his "short" hedged against the possibility that the entire market (and thus individual stocks) might move against his position. Jones, in fact, called his fund a "hedged fund" and objected to the term's bastardization into the now-common "hedge fund."

From the industry's beginnings in the mid-20th century, hedge funds grew at a relatively modest rate for the first quarter century, only passing $100 billion in assets under management (AUM) in the early 1990s. But thereafter the industry grew rapidly, passing $500 billion around 2000, and $1 trillion around 2004. The roughly 10,000 extant hedge funds now manage over $2 trillion. If these assets were distributed uniformly among funds—which they definitely are not—a typical fund would manage $200 million, and earn fees of several million dollars a year. No wonder they've piqued your interest!

How Hedge Funds Differ from Mutual Funds

Both types of funds represent pools of investors putting their capital in the hands of a manager. But mutual funds are far more transparent than hedge funds. Mutual funds have accepted SEC regulation as the price of having legal access to millions of small investors. Mutual funds must specify their strategies in their prospectus, and report their holdings and their results regularly.

Hedge funds, by contrast, are very lightly regulated. In the United States, restrictions imposed on investor qualifications serve to replace regulation: eligible investors must be "accredited," with levels of assets that put them in the upper few percent of American households. The implicit argument is that prosperous individuals can take care of themselves. Hedge funds are prohibited from advertising. (This may soon change, as outlined in the final chapter). In fact, many hedge fund managers shun publicity, in part to avoid any hint that they are engaged in backdoor advertising through the news. Hedge funds' original investors were wealthy individuals and families, but by the 1990s these were overtaken by large institutions such as charitable endowments and pension funds.

Hedge funds' legendary secretiveness goes far beyond skittishness about running afoul of the regulators. Finance is an industry where legally protecting intellectual property (like a new financial product or investing strategy) is virtually impossible, so secrecy is the only way to prevent (or more accurately, delay) competitors from copying your innovations. Hedge funds generally do not disclose their holdings and strategies publicly—and often report them to their investors only in the broadest terms, after the fact. Pulling back this curtain is one of the main motivations behind this book.

Hedge Fund Strategies

With thousands of funds, there are many possible ways to categorize their strategies. Strategies of many funds fall into four major types:

- *Equity*—where the emphasis is on stock selection. Many equity funds follow A. W. Jones's original long/short model.

- *Arbitrage*—where managers seek instances where price relationships between assets fall outside of normal variation, and bet on the relationship returning to normal. Early practitioners plied this trade in fixed income markets, but it now occurs in any market where quantitative analysis can identify price discrepancies to exploit.
- *Momentum or direction*—where managers have a macro view of the probable direction of prices in a market.
- *Event-driven*—trades instigated based on an event, such as a war, a supply disruption, or a merger. In the 1990s, "global macro" funds gained in prominence, mainly using event-driven strategies. Several prominent funds made their reputations in merger arbitrage.

This is only one way to categorize strategies; you will encounter others. Because the industry is relatively young and innovation is so continuous, no taxonomy will last long.

Managers can be long-only (they make money only if the asset rises in price), short-only (they profit only if the asset's price falls), or (most commonly) hedged (both long and short, although usually not equally). In addition, because the profits per transaction for many of these trades will be quite small proportionally, many hedge funds borrow extensively to "leverage" their investment. (UK investors refer to "leverage" as "gearing.") So a "130/30" equity strategy, for example, has gone long with 130 percent of available capital (by borrowing 30 percent over and above 100 percent equity capital), and has shorted 30 percent of the portfolio as a hedge.

Many of these distinctions will be elaborated in later chapters. Because the investing industry is so densely populated and so heavily compensated (as discussed later), there is intense competition to identify opportunities for likely profit. The original hedge funds operated mainly on experience and instinct: funds founded by Jones, Robertson, Michael Steinhardt, or Soros are each examples. By the 1990s, quantitative finance had matured as an academic discipline and computing power had become inexpensive enough that it was possible to examine many thousands of relationships among asset prices. The statistical work was often conducted by economists, physicists, or mathematicians, who collectively came to be termed "rocket scientists." Some of the foundations of this "quant" analysis approach will be introduced in this book.

Funds of Funds

Because hedge funds are barred from advertising (thereby making any search for a fund more challenging), choosing the right fund can be difficult for a client. Furthermore, the range of strategies is very wide, and intense competition among hedge funds and major Wall Street institutions can rapidly erode the effectiveness of any strategy. So institutional clients increasingly are turning to "funds of hedge funds"—managers who select the hedge funds into which to invest clients' money, monitor those funds' strategies and performance, and reallocate among funds as market conditions change. Funds of funds add their own fees on top of the fees charged by hedge funds themselves.

Hedge Fund Fees

Mutual funds cover their expenses based on an "expense ratio," measured as a percentage of assets under management. The median fund charges a bit more than 1 percent of assets each year. (Many funds also charge a "load"—a fee paid either at the time of original purchase or when the investor liquidates his holdings, known as a "front end load" or "back end load.") Note that the expense ratio is *not* dependent on performance—an investor pays it regardless of how his investment performed. This can be grating in a year when returns are negative: the investor is paying for the privilege of seeing their assets decline.

By contrast, hedge funds are compensated in a hybrid structure, with one part being a traditional expense ratio—usually 2 percent, not 1 percent —and the remainder being a portion of the fund's returns—customarily 20 percent. The 20 percent performance fee is of absolute performance, not for performance above a benchmark. This "2 and 20" fee arrangement is common, identical to that in private equity firms (investment firms that buy a privately held company and improve its operations in order to sell it later at a profit, usually in a public stock offering). However, it is not a universal standard: Funds with superior reputations may charge much more. In its heyday, Renaissance Capital's Medallion Fund charged 5 percent annually and 44 percent of returns, and we've heard of incentive fees as high as 55 percent of returns. However, as the industry has become more crowded and its downside protection was sorely tested in the 2008 market meltdown, some firms are dropping their fees to as low as 1 percent annually plus 10 percent performance fee.

These fees have been sufficient to make many hedge fund founders billionaires. Sometimes they have earned it, generated annual returns of the long term well in excess of 20 percent annually (well over twice the return of most stock indexes). But since the industry as a whole has disappointed lately, critics argue that hedge funds overcharge and underdeliver.

How Hedge Funds are Evaluated (I): Return

The core issues in evaluating any investment are return and risk.

Return is straightforward: Compare the value of holdings at the end of a time period (a year, or a day) to the value at the beginning. In mathematical terms

Return = [Value (t)/Value $(t-1)$] − 1, where (t) indicates a time period.

Example:

  Value (t) = \$110
 Value $(t-1)$ = \$100
   Return = [\$110/\$100] − 1 = 1.1 − 1 = .1 = 10%.

For much of this book, we will be considering daily returns. Commonly, to compare investments, returns are annualized, converting days to years. This is done by compounding the daily return by the number of trading days in a year, 252 as follows (in Python):

annual_return = cumprod(daily_returns+1) − 1

There are 260 weekdays in a 52-week year, but generally markets are closed for about 8 days each year for holidays.

Since money left in a growing asset compounds (like interest), the right way to compute an annual return over several years is the *compound annual growth rate* (CAGR). Say, your portfolio was worth \$200 in 2012, after starting at $100 in 2002. That's a 100 percent *cumulative return* over 10 years. But the annual return is not simply [100 percent/10 years] or 10 percent because that computation ignores the compounding effect.

Compounding over multiple years is captured by raising an annual return to an exponent, representing the number of years that the return compounds (in this case, 10 years). In the aforementioned example

$$\$200 = \$100 \times (1 + \text{annual return}) \wedge 10$$

Since annual return, or CAGR, is unknown, we must rearrange this equation:

$$[\$200/100] = (1 + \text{CAGR}) \wedge 10$$
$$2 = (1 + \text{CAGR}) \wedge 10$$
$$2\wedge(1/10) = 1 + \text{CAGR}$$
$$\text{Since } 2 \wedge 1/10 = 1.072, \text{ then}$$
$$1.072 = 1 + \text{CAGR, and}$$
$$\text{CAGR} = 7.2\% \text{ (i.e., } 1.072 - 1)$$

So a portfolio that grows at 7.2 percent on average each year will double in size in 10 years. We use the term *CAGR* to remind us that we need to reflect the effects of compounding in computing annual returns. In this instance, the effect of compounding was substantial: 7.2 percent compound annual growth was enough to double a portfolio in 10 years, whereas it would need to grow at 10 percent annual if the growth process was "simple" (not compounded).

Compounding, and exponential math, is very difficult to develop intuitively or to mentally calculate easily. We chose this example to introduce you to your new best friend: the *Rule of 72*. It is an approximation of compounding. This rule states that you can approximate the number of periods that will be needed for a sum to double by dividing the CAGR (in whole numbers) into the number 72. A portfolio growing at 8 percent will need about 9 years to double, because 8 × 9 = 72. At 6 percent CAGR, 12 years will be required to double (6 × 12 = 72). Similarly, you can infer a CAGR if you know the starting and ending values of a portfolio and the time elapsed. So if a portfolio doubled over 15 years, you know that its CAGR was a bit less than 5 percent; specifically, 4.8 percent (15 × 5 = 75; 15 × 4.8 = 72).

Wall Street interviewers routinely ask the interviewee compounding math problems that most people cannot calculate mentally without a shortcut like this. It is also effective for portfolio growth that is a multiple of two, even a large one. For example, an asset that grew from $100 to $400 has grown four-fold, or 2 × 2 (2 ^ 2); to $800 is eight-fold (2 ^ 3), and so forth. This can be very helpful when considering portfolio growth over long time periods: A 100-fold increase is a bit less than 2 ^ 7; 1000-fold is almost exactly 2 ^ 10 (2 ^ 10 = 1,024).

Hedge funds typically receive an incentive or performance fee based on return: 20 percent of the investor's return over and above a 2 percent management fee. So, for example, if the hedge fund returns 4 percent in a year, the fund managers will receive 2 percent fee plus (0.2 × [4% − 2%] = 0.4%), or a total compensation of 2.4 percent of AUM. In that example, the managers kept 60 percent of the portfolio's return (2.4%/4%). If the portfolio earned 10 percent in a year, the fund's compensation would be 2 percent plus [0.2 × (10% − 2%) = 1.6%], or 36 percent of the portfolio's return. In other words, all (100 percent) the first 2 percent of the portfolio's return goes to the fund manager, then 20 percent of any returns above 2 percent. Note that if the portfolio's returns are negative, the manager will earn no incentive fee, but the 2 percent management fee will represent far more than the (negative) return the client earned.

As you can see, hedge fund fees are very generous to fund managers.

How Hedge Funds Are Evaluated (II): Return Versus Benchmark (Relative Return)

Compensating managers based on absolute return implies that no positive return could have been earned otherwise: that the only alternative would be to put your money under your mattress. But realistically, investors have a vast array of alternatives, from short-term fixed income instruments such as commercial paper or treasury bills to a range of equities (stocks). Investment managers are commonly compared to a *benchmark:* a nonmanaged investment that presents a relevant comparator. For funds that invest in equities, the most common benchmark is a stock *index* such as the S&P 500 (the 500 largest companies, measured by market capitalization, traded on U.S. stock exchanges). Funds that use narrower strategies can be compared to narrower and more pertinent indexes or a weighted combination of more than one index (with the weights based on the asset class weights in the strategy). Finally, a few research firms such as Hedge Fund Research, Inc. compile an index of hedge fund performance (HFRX). However, this index has significant drawbacks, which are outlined later.

Decades of financial academic research, drawn mainly, although not solely, from mutual funds, has demonstrated that very few active investment managers produce consistent performance that exceeds their benchmark. (Exceeding a benchmark constitutes *alpha*, a measure of investing skill, defined later.) This is a major investor relations problem for active managers: Activity imposes management and trading costs, which are only justified if they produce superior returns to "passive" (unmanaged) investing. Many studies by finance academics have found such justification very hard to come by: Active management at best matches, and more typically underperforms, benchmark indexes *before* management costs. Frequent trading—common for active managers—and fees pose a considerable further drag.

With hedge funds, those fees are significantly higher than with mutual funds. Studies of hedge funds have found that managers can frequently generate positive alpha (outperform their benchmark), but their compensation absorbs at least half of the portfolio's annual excess return over the benchmark. One recent analysis found that over the life of the industry for which performance data were available (1998 to 2010), managers absorbed between 84 and 98 percent of the total profits earned. In other words, clients kept only one-fiftieth to one-sixth of total return. And in one-fourth of those years, total profits were negative— but fund managers were still paid 2 percent of AUM. John Bogle, the founder of Vanguard mutual funds, which originated indexed investment, has famously said about mutual funds that investors "get what they *don't* pay for." The analog for hedge funds would be "no gain without at least equal pain": investors will pay high fees regardless, so that in a good year they will share returns about equally with their managers. In a bad year, the client will bear all of the pain—negative returns, depressed further by the 2 percent management fee.

How Hedge Funds Are Evaluated (III): Risk

Hedge funds' rationale is not solely to maximize return but also to control risk—that's the reason for the term "hedge." Risk is operationalized as **volatility** of a portfolio's returns. Figure 2.1 illustrates two portfolios of differing volatility: the Dow Jones Industrial Average (an index of 30 stocks) versus a particular fund, over the period from March 2009 to July 2012. Both earned similar cumulative returns (a cumulative 43 percent for the Dow and 33 percent for the fund, or 11.6 percent and 9.2 percent annually, respectively), but the fund did so with significantly less volatility: short-term spikes and dips in price were less frequent and less pronounced. This is what investors seek when they pay for hedge fund management: reduced volatility.

The most common statistical measure of volatility is the *standard deviation* in per-period returns. Standard deviations are the square root of the sum of the squared deviations in per period prices versus the mean for all periods in the sample. If a given mean daily return was 0.1 percent and return on June 1 was 0.3 percent, its squared deviation (also known as "variance") for the day would be .04% = 0.2% $\wedge$ 2. (The squaring is to correct for negative values—days when the portfolio shrank in value.) For the two portfolios discussed in the previous paragraph, the Dow's standard deviation was 1.23 percent and the fund's was 0.58 percent— the fund was less than half as volatile as the index.

Figure 2.1 Price of fund versus benchmark, 2009 to 2012

Source: Courtesy Lucena Research, LLC

Critics argue that standard deviation is a measure that only an academic could love, because it does not differentiate upward deviations—the kind we seek!—from downward deviations. "Drawdown" is a supplemental measure often used to address this. It is simply the maximum drop from peak to trough, measured as a percentage of the peak level. The Sortino ratio focuses on the downside, whereas the more commonly used Sharpe ratio is indifferent between upward and downward deviations.

Sharpe Ratio: Combining Return and Risk

The Capital Asset Pricing Model, discussed in Chapter 7, observes that across different asset classes it is virtually impossible to increase return without also increasing risk. This unavoidable trade-off between risk and return encourages us to consider measures that combine the two: one that we wish to maximize, and one we wish to minimize. Among different portfolios (or different managers), which one offers the lowest risk for a given return or the highest return for a given risk? This is analogous to "cost–benefit analysis" in public projects: Scarce resources mandate that we spend them on those that will produce the most benefit per dollar, or that will produce a given benefit most cheaply.

Nobel Prize winner William Sharpe developed his namesake ratio to measure the efficiency of a portfolio in these terms. The *Sharpe Ratio* puts return—the thing we wish to maximize—in the numerator and risk—what we want to minimize, as measured by the standard deviation of the portfolio's return—in the denominator. The only wrinkle is that "return" is excess return above the risk-free rate—usually the rate offered by short-term Treasury bills. (This is because we can get that return with no risk at all.) The formula is therefore:

Sharpe Ratio = (*r*[portfolio] – *r* [risk free])/standard deviation (portfolio)

As an example, the long-term (since 1926) nominal return for the S&P 500 has been close to 10 percent. During this period, the average risk-free rate has been about 2.5 percent. The S&P 500's standard deviation has been about 15 percent. So its Sharpe Ratio over the past 80 years has been:

$$(10\% - 2.5\%)/15\% = 7.5\%/15\% = 0.5$$

High Sharpe ratios indicate high return per unit of risk, so 0.5 doesn't look particularly appealing, but you'll need to calculate this figure for some other assets or time periods to put it in perspective. (A value of 1.0 can be thought of very loosely as being fairly compensated for risk—that is, each unit of risk generates an equal number of units of return. But a less loose interpretation of the Sharpe Ratio is simply that higher numbers are better than lower ones. It is important to note that Sharpe ratios at or above 1.0 are *very* uncommon.) For the two portfolios mentioned earlier, their Sharpe ratios were, respectively, .63 for the Dow and .94 for the fund. So on a risk-adjusted basis, the fund was superior by about half again over the Dow.

Drawdown ratios and Sortino ratios measure a portfolio's exposure to downdrafts and are especially relevant to hedge funds, whose *raison d'etre* is that they aspire to minimize falls in down markets, at the cost of reduced upside exposure in rising markets.

CHAPTER 3

An Illustrative Hedge Fund Strategy: Arbitrage

After long/short "hedged" trading strategies, the next most common hedge fund strategy is *arbitrage*. In its original form, arbitrage meant earning a profit by exploiting discrepancies in the price of an identical good in two different markets. For instance, due to a glut of oil in the American Midwest in 2012 and 2013, the price of oil (dollars per barrel) differed in the Brent (North Sea) market from the Texas market, with the Brent price being as much as several dollars per barrel higher. Arbitrageurs could make a profit by buying Texas oil and selling Brent oil. In this sense, all retailers are arbitrageurs; in that, they buy a product from a manufacturer or wholesaler and sell it to retail customers at a higher price.

Traditionally, arbitrage refers to strategies that operate on the same asset in two different time periods or at the same time in two different markets. Some fixed-income arbitrageurs exploit price disparities in nearly identical issues. For example, one of LTCM's (Long Term Capital Management's) most successful strategies involved buying Treasury bills in the secondary market some days after they were issued, and shorting new bills of the same maturity. This exploited the fact that newly issued bills are the most liquid and carry a liquidity premium. As they age, that premium evaporates, and their price can overshoot downward. Shorting new bills exploited their overpricing, and going long older bills exploited their underpricing.

Similar opportunities can exist among equities. For instance, Company A may own a large position in Company B, but if other factors are depressing A's stock price, it may be possible to effectively own shares in B at a lower price (by buying A's shares) than buying them directly. Owning shares in Royal Dutch Shell has occasionally been an economical way of owning its two parents.

The term "arbitrage" has taken on a broader meaning over time, applying to a wider range of opportunities.

It is not necessary that we arbitrage between prices for the same asset at different exchanges. Such strategies can be named after the instruments traded (e.g., commodities, fixed income, or equities) or the technique used to identify the arbitrage opportunity (e.g., statistical arbitrage, or "stat arb").

Statistical arbitrage refers to those investing strategies that seek to identify and exploit instances where the market price of an asset has (temporarily) deviated from its *true* price, or its intrinsic value. In this case the arbitrage is between the true price and the market price. Market prices above intrinsic value can be expected to fall, which suggests a short position. Prices below intrinsic value offer an opportunity to make money in a long position.

If a market is reasonably efficient (efficient markets are discussed in Chapter 8), such opportunities will be fleeting because investors will quickly bid up the price of undervalued assets, and bid down the price of overpriced assets. In other words, investors will "arbitrage away" these inefficiencies.

Another form of statistical arbitrage is based on a phenomenon called *regression to the mean*. An asset with a volatile price that is driven away from true value will in time return to its "mean" true value—how quickly it returns indicates the market's efficiency.

Value investing is another type of arbitrage that entails taking long positions in assets that the investor considers underpriced, in the expectation that price will eventually be bid up to the near-true value. Warren Buffett is the best-known value investor practicing today. Short investing is the opposite: taking short positions on assets the investor considers overpriced. David Einhorn is a well-known "short."

As in many other strategies, profit margins are small and opportunities may be rapidly competed away by other arbitrageurs. For these reasons, hedge funds often leverage extensively to maximize the volume of trades they can undertake, and use programmed or high-frequency trading systems to act on opportunities very quickly.

Bio: Steven Cohen, SAC Capital

Born: 1956

Firm: SAC Capital Advisers, Stamford, CT

Founded: 1992

Style: Equity arbitrage

How it Differentiates: Like Ray Dalio's Bridgewater, an intensely combative culture intended to generate the best ideas through extreme competition. Cohen believes that conviction and speed are critical to SAC's competitive advantage. He routinely makes very large bets—10 percent of the portfolio or more—very quickly. He believes that the alpha associated with an investing idea dissipates (i.e., is arbitraged away) within 20 days of its discovery. His firm has been accused of relying on inside information for much of its competitive advantage (see further text).

AUM: Peaked at $15 billion in early 2013; about $11 billion in summer of 2013; expected to fall to about $9 billion in 2014, all from founder and employees. Reductions due to client redemptions following insider trading criminal charges (see further text).

Cohen's background: Cohen, the son of a dress manufacturer and part-time piano teacher, grew up in Long Island. He attended Wharton, graduating in 1978. His first job was as a junior options arbitrage trader at Gruntal & Co., rising quickly by 1984 to lead a team of traders that generated an average $100,000 profit per day. He left Gruntal in 1992 to found SAC with

$20 million in personal funds. In 2013 Cohen was estimated to be worth over $9 billion dollars, among the richest Americans. He was also on Time *magazine and* Bloomberg Businessweek's *lists of the most influential Americans.*

Insider trading indictment: In the spring of 2013, SAC Capital was indicted by the SEC for insider trading. Cohen required all "high conviction" trade ideas to be approved by him personally; many are alleged to be based on information from insiders at the traded companies. Five former SAC traders were also indicted, and three have confessed as of August 2013. Cohen is under administrative review by the SEC but has not been charged.

Color: Cohen has spent hundreds of millions on Impressionist and contemporary art, including a landscape *entitled "Police Gazette" by artist* Willem de Kooning *for $63.5 million; and $25 million each for a* Warhol *and a* Picasso. *In 2006, Cohen attempted to make the most expensive art purchase in history when he offered to purchase* Picasso's Le Reve *from casino mogul* Steve Wynn *for $139 million. Just days before the painting was to be transported to Cohen, Wynn, who suffers from poor vision due to* retinitis pigmentosa, *accidentally thrust his elbow through the painting while showing it to a group of acquaintances inside of his office at* Wynn Las Vegas. *The purchase was canceled, and Wynn still held the painting until early November 2012, when Cohen purchased the painting for $150 million.*

CHAPTER 4

Market-Making Mechanics

The basis for any investment market is just that—a market. *Markets* are locations (physical or virtual) where sellers and customers convene to exchange goods, or in our case, financial instruments. If you've ever watched business news on television, you've probably seen a shot of the New York Stock Exchange (NYSE)—often companies stage publicity events where a representative rings the bell to open the day's trading before the cameras. In the NYSE, shares of stock in U.S.-listed companies are exchanged. Prices of each exchange are tracked to reveal trends in interest in those shares—rising prices indicate rising appeal (more buyers than sellers), while falling prices indicate the opposite.

Investors do not occupy the NYSE, or other exchanges, themselves. They transact their exchanges through intermediaries. Brokerage firms interface with end-buyers and end-sellers. Those brokers, in turn, trade with market makers, who facilitate the trades. At the NYSE, the market makers are called *specialists* and they are the only entities who transact business on the floor of the exchange. In some markets like the NASDAQ, there is no floor—all trading occurs electronically—and therefore no specialists.

Market Spreads

Most of the time there is a small difference between the price at which a buyer may purchase a stock, termed the *bid price*, and the price at which a seller will sell the stock, the *ask price*. At a given moment an instrument therefore has two prices: bid and ask. For example, IBM might be quoted as "$200.50 ask; $199.75 bid." The difference between these two prices is known as the *market spread*, and represents the profit opportunity that induces brokerages and specialists to make the market—to connect sellers and buyers.

Markets with high trading volumes will attract more market makers, who will compete with each other based on the price they charge to handle a transaction—that is, based on the spread they charge. Highly liquid markets (with large trading volumes and numerous market makers) tend to have the smallest spreads. In fact, widening spreads can be an early indication of a market whose liquidity is freezing up, as occurred in the fixed income markets in the fall of 2008. Niche markets, such as instruments traded in frontier markets such as Myanmar or Kazakhstan, have low volumes and consequently wide market spreads.

Types of Order (Basic)

Investors enter *buy* and *sell* orders with their brokers for a certain number of shares (*round lots* are 100 shares). Each of these may be either "at the market" (a *market order*), where the broker simply accepts whatever price the market is offering; or a *limit order*, which sets a condition before the order can be executed. For example, a buy "limit order for 100 IBM at $200" instructs the broker to buy 100 IBM shares only if he can do so at a price of $200 per share or less. The equivalent limit order to sell instructs the broker to sell only if the price is $200 or higher.

Types of Order (Intermediate)

Although exchanges only accept and execute buy and sell orders in the exchange's order book (as described in the next section), other more complex orders can be established, with the added complexity handled by a broker. Two examples are *selling short* and *stop orders*.

Selling short is a bet that a stock's price will fall. (The conventional bet, that a stock's price will rise, is termed *going long*.) The investor borrows shares from a holder and sells them, earning the proceeds of the sale. At a later point, they buy the same number of shares and return them to their lender. If the shares fell in price from the earlier sale price, the investor pockets the difference. If it rises, they lose the difference. In addition, the investor who is shorting must pay interest to the owner of the shares borrowed—a fee known as the rebate—as well as any dividends to which the owner is entitled during the borrowing period.

Shorting, then, involves two transactions: "sell to open" (to open the short position) and "buy to close." Their order in time is the reverse of that in a normal long transaction. Shorts are considered riskier than longs, on average, for several reasons. First, the long-term trend in stock prices is upward, so a short bet must be premised on the belief that the stock in question will move in a contrary direction. Second, the potential loss is unbounded. The maximum loss with a long position is 100 percent—the stock's price can't go below zero. But the theoretical maximum loss for a short is unlimited, since a stock's price can rise without boundary. Finally, executives in companies being shorted do not take kindly to it. If the investor relies on access to the company (e.g., a brokerage firm's analysts who cover the company), the company may retaliate by curtailing access by those analysts. Not surprisingly, few hedge funds are short-only, although many use shorts to hedge long positions. Shorts require exceptionally deep research to identify overvalued stocks, and an iron determination to be contrarian.

Stop orders are contingent orders, usually used for risk management. *Stop loss* orders are the most common type. An investor might instruct one's broker to place a market order automatically if the price of the stock falls more than a specified threshold (e.g., 25 percent) below the purchase price. *Trailing stops* act equivalently, but make the condition the most recent high to preserve most of the gains for an asset whose price has risen since original purchase. Less commonly, investors may sell a portion of their position to preserve partial gains; a *free ride*, for example, specifies that the broker should sell half of a position when it has doubled in price from original purchase. That way the original capital is "taken off the table," and only profits are at risk. Each of these more complex or contingent orders must be placed through a broker. Some investors believe that stop loss orders constitute important information that other market participants can exploit (as illustrated in a later section), so they advise keeping stop loss rules private (i.e., withholding from a broker until it is time to execute).

Matching Orders: The Order Book

As investors place orders in the market, specialists (or the exchange computer system) tabulate an ever-changing order book. An example is shown in Figure 4.1.

Bid size	Price	Ask size
	$100.10	300
	$100.05	300
	$100.00	200
100	$99.95	
50	$99.90	
100	$99.85	

Figure 4.1 Sample order book for XYZ stock

Orders are grouped as Buy or Sell; noting the number of shares being offered (ask) and requested (bid) at each possible price. The spread is the difference between the lowest ask price and the highest bid price—in this instance, 5 cents (0.05 dollars), or 0.5 percent of the midpoint between bid and ask. This very small spread is an indication of a very liquid market.

If a seller places a market order for 150 shares, it would be filled by combining buy orders that cumulate to that many shares, starting from the highest buy order (in this case, for 100 shares at $99.95) and adding additional buy orders until all 150 shares have been absorbed. In this instance, the next-highest buy order, for 50 shares at $99.90, would also be utilized. The seller's average price per share would be $99.933. Economically, this sale has moved the equilibrium price of XYZ a short distance down the demand curve: the next buyer will only bid $99.85 for XYZ. A purchase will move in the opposite direction, up the demand curve. So if the preponderance of trades is sales, prices will fall, and if most are purchases, they will rise. Equal numbers of shares bought and sold should result in stable prices. In the example in Figure 4.1, there is a higher volume of XYZ shares on offer than there are bids for them, which suggests that XYZ's share price will probably decline. As you can see, knowledge of the order book can provide useful information for predicting short-term price changes.

The Advantage of Milliseconds

Trades aren't always cleared on exchanges. A brokerage firm that simultaneously holds overlapping buy and sell orders from different clients may clear them internally. This saves the firm exchange fees; further, the broker can earn the market maker's spread. In the past decade, syndicates of brokerage firms have created "dark pools"—essentially informal exchanges among those firms. Market making specialists may likewise clear trades before they are submitted to the formal exchange.

As the example in Figure 4.1 illustrates, discrepancies in the volume of sell versus buy orders can predict short-term price trends. So brokers and market makers possess important information on which they can trade. The key is speed, since orders change constantly and new orders will change the balance of trading volumes between sell and buy orders. For this reason, firms have invested heavily in automating trading systems (since computers can execute trades far faster than people can), and in minimizing the time it takes to communicate trade orders to their recipients. Time can be saved with better communications technology, such as replacing copper wire with fiber optic cable; or by locating the trading platforms closer to the receiving entities, such as co-locating the platform at the exchange itself. Competitive advantage can hinge on milliseconds. Several books have covered "high frequency trading" (HFT), including most recently Lewis's *Flash Boys*.

Front running is one where a broker issues trades in advance of those of its clients, knowing the price movements that will probably occur when clients' orders are executed. Its ethics are dubious when a broker is trading against its own clients, but fair game when the counterparty is another broker's client. Reducing (through technology or colocation) the time to see an opportunity and execute a transaction is sanctioned front-running. Processing large numbers of trades very quickly to exploit evident short-term price trends is at the core of trading-oriented hedge funds' strategies, and provides ample opportunities for IT professionals.

CHAPTER 5

Introduction to Company Valuation

A successful investment indicates that the buyer had a more accurate view of the asset's true value than the seller had (otherwise, the seller would have demanded a higher price). The reverse is true for failed investments. This implies that different market participants have different views of the value of an asset, like a company's stock. (Remember that a share of company stock is simply partial ownership of the entire company.) In fact, it is this mixture of views that enables a market to work.

This suggests that investing opportunities appear when an investor spots an asset whose current price diverges from what he believes is its true value. Financial markets may be quite efficient—that is, they may rapidly reflect most relevant information that affect an asset's value in its current market price—but hedge funds and other investors seek to make money from these occasional differences, or inefficiencies. (Market efficiency or inefficiency will be treated in a later chapter). If the current price is below estimated true value, it presents an opportunity to go long on that asset; if the asset is presently overpriced, it presents a short opportunity.

Successful investors develop and apply techniques that independently value companies to discover discrepancies between price and value. The first popular book on "value investing," Benjamin Graham's *The Intelligent Investor* (often cited by Graham protégé Warren Buffett as the definitive work on this investing style), argued that investors should seek a *margin of safety*—that is, they should only buy stocks whose price was well below the investor's estimate of their true value. This has been called "buying dollar bills for fifty cents." But value investing is only possible if the investor is confident of his or her own personal estimate of true value. This chapter is an introduction to valuation techniques.

The methods that follow are often called *fundamental analysis*, because they are based on the fundamentals of a company's business operations and finances. These methods are distinct from *technical analysis*, which attempts to predict stock prices based on past price behavior. Technical analysis also is known more descriptively as "charting."

We will cover three key methods for estimating the value of a company using fundamental factors:

- Book value: An estimate based on the sum of assets and liabilities of the company
- Intrinsic value: An estimate based on future dividends to be paid by the company
- Earnings growth: Projection of expanded earnings into the future

Asset-Based Valuation: Book Value

Companies are required to periodically report their assets and their liabilities, with the difference between the two constituting the firm's net worth. Assets are productive items the firm owns, which can be tangible assets such as factories, or intangible assets such as patents. Assets are categorized according to how quickly they can be converted into cash. Liabilities are financial obligations the firm has undertaken: debts, commitments to pay for raw materials, employment contracts, and so forth; they are likewise categorized by their duration into the future. If the firm closed its doors tomorrow, its net worth is the best available approximation of what its owners would be left with after selling off its assets and paying off its obligations. On the balance sheet this is shown as stockholder's equity or *book value*: it is the value of the firm as captured by accountants on its books.

Book value can diverge from *market value*—the value of the firm as appraised by market prices, also known as *market capitalization*—for several reasons. First, accounting rules are biased to be conservative, so even if an asset has risen in value since the firm originally purchased it—say, a piece of real estate in a growing city—it will be carried on the balance sheet at its original price, less accumulated depreciation. This deflates book value relative to the firm's intrinsic value. For these reasons, the reported book value is usually below the price the company is worth if it were actually liquidated. However, if the firm is forced to sell an asset involuntarily—such as in bankruptcy—it may receive far less than what it had paid, especially if the sale is forced by bad economic conditions that depress the price of all assets. So, in a recession, book value may overstate true value.

When using book value for investing purposes, an asset-based assessment would compare a company's book value—possibly adjusted if the investor believes it is inflated or depressed by special conditions—to its market capitalization. On a per-share basis, the investor would compute the *price-to-book ratio*:

Price-to-book ratio = share price/book value per share

Mature companies with few growth prospects (discussed in further text), or troubled companies that may face liquidation, may have a share price below book value, or little above it. That is, a price-to-book ratio of less than 1.0 or barely above 1.0. Conservative value–style investors are attracted when they can buy a share for less than its book value; this is not uncommon if the company, its industry, or the entire economy is in distress.

Intrinsic Value: Dividend-Based Valuation

Companies exist to use assets in such a way that their value grows over time. This is one of the reasons why book value may underestimate the company's true value: Book value does not reflect future prospects. Capturing this element of value requires us to examine one of the fundamental concepts in finance: the time value of money.

Time Value of Money

Assets are more valuable if they generate cash into the future. If I buy that asset from you, cash flows you received while you owned it will now be paid to me. But I will probably pay you a single lump sum to gain ownership, a sum that is likely far more than one year of cash flows. So the price we negotiate must somehow convert a stream of future cash flows—that the seller relinquishes and the buyer expects—into a lump sum. This process is called *discounting* to reflect the *time value of money.*

Money's time value can be illustrated with a simple example. Say your friend is scheduled to receive a sum of money in one year—for instance, when his deceased grandfather's estate is settled. He can document with certainty that he will receive $10,000 one year from today. But he needs money now. He offers to sell you his right to that bequest. What would you pay for it?

Certainly less than $10,000. Your first reaction is probably that you can't be certain that something won't go wrong and deny you the transferred bequest, so you need to lower your price to reflect that uncertainty. That's an absolutely correct reaction; but for simplicity's sake, let's assume that there is absolutely no doubt that the $10,000 will be forthcoming in 1 year. Is this asset—your purchased claim on the grandfather's estate—worth $10,000 to you?

Again, almost certainly not. Why? Because whatever sum you spend to buy this claim can't be used for some other productive purpose—to deposit in a bank, to start a business, or to buy shares in an existing business. If you buy your friend's promissory note due in 1 year, you lose the use of your money for 1 year. The lost opportunity—which economists call, literally, "opportunity cost"—is the return that you've sacrificed by failing to make the best alternative investment. Let's say that the alternative is to buy shares in the S&P 500 ETF, SPY, which you expect will return 10 percent over the next year. Then your friend's note is only attractive if its expected return is at least as good.

We "charge" the proposed investment—your friend's promissory note, $10,000 payable in 1 year—for the opportunity that you are sacrificing to invest in SPY and earn 10 percent. We *discount* the expected $10,000 payout in 1 year by 10 percent per year to express that *future value* as a value in the present or *present value.* Specifically,

Present value = future value/(1 + discount rate) ^ (number of years till payment)

$PV = FV/(1 + DR) \wedge I$

$PV = \$10,000/(1.1) \wedge 1$

$PV = \$9,090.91$

Where I is the number of years until payment. So you should not pay more than roughly $9,091 for the promissory note. The *discount rate,* shown as DR, is the rate of return the investor could receive from investing in the best alternative asset. We used the example of the stock market, but others often use a less risky investment such as the interest rate on Treasury bonds. The discount rate chosen should reflect the lost opportunity associated with most likely alternative investment. We charge that opportunity cost to this investment by discounting it to reflect the time value of money we are sacrificing by investing here.

Assets can offer either a single payment, like the aforementioned promissory note, or a stream of payments. Stocks differ from bonds or promissory notes in that they may provide a stream of payments in the form of dividends. These dividends will be paid on a regular basis into the infinite future as long as the company's board elects to maintain the dividend. Note, however, that not all companies pay dividends, and, of course, sometimes companies suspend dividends or fail completely.

Accordingly, assessing the value of a stock based on those future dividend payments is a bit more complex. The present value of all the future dividend payments is equivalent to the present value of each payment, added together.

To explain this, let's go back to the example of promissory notes: If you bought two promissory notes—one payable in 1 year, and the other offering $10,000 payable in 2 years—the value of that portfolio would be the sum of the present values of each note:

PV note 1 (due in 1 year): $10,000/(1.1) ^ 1 = $9,090.91
PV note 2 (due in 2 years): $10,000/(1.1) ^ 2 = $8,264.46
Portfolio value (sum of each note's PV) = $17,355.37

The *intrinsic value* of any asset is simply the present value of all future returns. This is true whether the returns are a single payment or multiple payments, uniform in amount (as in this example), or nonuniform.

The math of discounting to compute the present value is straightforward if the future payments are constant. A challenge is in estimating the future value cash flows, which is outside this book's scope. So we will illustrate valuing a share of stock with simple constant cash flows: dividends.

The Dividend Discount Model

Say that you own a share in an electric utility company, Divco, which pays $1 per year in dividends. Also assume that your best alternative use of your capital offered a return of 8 percent per year. Then the value of the stream of dividends over 10 years from Divco would be as follows:

Year 1: $\$1/(1.08) \wedge 1 = \$0.9259$

Year 2: $\$1/(1.08) \wedge 2 = \$0.8573$

Year 3: $\$1/(1.08) \wedge 3 = \$.07938$

.

.

.

Year 10: $\$1/(1.08) \wedge 10 = \$0.4632$

The total value of this 10-year stream of dividends is simply the sum of these ten present values, or $6.71. If the only returns to shareholders were this constant stream of dividends for 10 years, a share of Divco stock would have an intrinsic value of $6.71. If it traded in the market for $7.00, it would be overpriced. If it sold for $5.00 a share, it would be a bargain.

Note that each successive year's dividend is worth less in the present, because each dividend is paid farther in the future. By year 10, one dollar in dividends a decade hence is worth less than half as much today. However, dividends don't usually end after 10 years. What if we extended payments farther in the future? For example, a $1.00 dividend payable 50 years from now would today be worth as follows:

Year 50: $\$1/(1.08) \wedge 50 = \$0.0213$

... or barely 1/50th of its future value of $1.

Long-Term Ownership of an Asset

You can see that if you extend the time horizon far enough into the future, the present value of a dividend then is effectively zero today. So an infinite time horizon won't generate an infinite present value, since beyond some time horizon the present value of future cash flows will be as close to zero as to be negligible. Still those future payments do have value, so how can we compute it?

Ownership of an income-producing asset means, in principle, that you will receive payments *in perpetuity*. (This applies, for example, to any stock: as long as the company survives, its owners receive its earnings.) Consider our earlier equation for a single payment I years in the future:

$$PV = FV/(1 + DR) \wedge I$$

We're looking for the sum of all these future values, so we can take advantage of the solution to the infinite sum

$$\sum_{i=1}^{\infty} \frac{1}{n^i} = \frac{1}{n-1} \text{ where } |n| > 1$$

And substitute $(1 + DR)$ for n in the equation to get:

$$PV = FV/((1 + DR) - 1)$$
$$PV = FV/DR$$

The value of a perpetuity—that is, a stream of equal payments forever—is simply the payment (we will use D for dividend now instead of FV) divided by the discount rate. Thus, the PV of perpetuity of payments of D each year is D/DR. In the Divco example, the present value of a share of Divco stock paying $1.00 in dividends each year forever (assuming an 8 percent DR) is

$$PV \text{ (Divco share)} = \$1.00/.08 = \$12.50$$

So more than half of the share's total value will be realized within the first 10 years,

since PV (10 years) = $6.71, while
PV (forever) = $12.50.

Said differently, all of the dividends paid from years 11 to infinity are worth $5.79.

Growth-Based Valuations

Fast-growing assets, like small growth companies, are valued based on the projections of (fast growing) future earnings. The methods used are identical to those mentioned in the previous sections. The difference is that each year's earnings are projected to be higher than the previous years. The company's value is the sum of each year's discounted cashflow (i.e., present value). In theory, this could be infinity, but, in practice, for any reasonable discount rate, cash flows many years in the future will be discounted essentially to zero. This is why a perpetual cash flow still has a finite present value.

Of course, valuations will depend critically on the assumed rate of growth in earnings. Small differences in growth assumptions can lead to big disparities in valuations.

Integrating Asset-Based and Cash Flow–Based Valuations

The mathematics is the easy part; the challenging part is all the judgments that must be made to create the inputs and assumptions used in these calculations.

Usually asset-based estimates produce lower valuations than do those based on long-term discounted cash flows. This is because asset-based valuations are based mainly on past prices paid for assets, not the—hopefully—enhanced value they have achieved from their use (hopefully superior) by the company. But even book value can overestimate company value if the conditions of sale are not conducive to getting a good price—like a forced liquidation, or a bad recession. Asset-based calculations are often viewed as "lower bounds," but even they may need to be adjusted downward in distress sale circumstances. Analysts commonly discount book value by 30 percent or 50 percent to represent what they believe is the true "worst case."

Cash flow–based estimates are slightly more involved, since it may be necessary to compute, and then discount, future cash flow for each of a number of years. Clearly, the farther in the future you project, the more conjectural your projection will be, since the number of intervening surprises can only increase. You can be reassured that forecasting errors have declining importance farther in the future, because their present values will be more heavily discounted.

An asset-based valuation implicitly ignores future earnings; while a cash flow–based valuation focuses exclusively on those future earnings. Adding the two together can produce the most complete valuation.

Analysts commonly produce a range of valuations. Different methods (such as asset- vs. cash flow–based methods) produce different values, as just noted. Different assumptions will likewise cause variations in values.

What If?

As an example, say, Divco is building a new power plant in an undeveloped area expected to experience rapid population growth (and therefore growth in demand for electric power). The investor might develop several scenarios, reflecting different hypothetical growth rates (and therefore rates of growth in power sales). The "base case" reflects the expected future—say, 4 percent annual population growth for 10 years, tapering to 1 percent per year thereafter. But the investor would be prudent to consider an alternative, more pessimistic scenario, of, say, 2 percent for 10 years and 0 percent annually thereafter. The optimistic scenario might produce a value several times the pessimistic scenario.

For asset-based valuations, an optimistic scenario might assume that each asset will be sold for full book value, and a pessimistic scenario might assume, say, 50 percent of book.

So with several possible valuations—different methods, and different scenarios—which one is right? There is no way to know until the future unfolds. Investors commonly consider a *range* of value estimates. If they are aggressive, they will emphasize the high end; if conservative, the low end. Graham argued for a margin of safety—emphasizing the low end, or possibly something even lower.

In the interests of simplicity, many Wall Street analysts produce a single, point-estimate "target price," but that is really substituting precision for accuracy. All of us have been "mugged by reality"—surprised by developments, usually on the downside, that made a mockery of optimistic valuations. (Dramatic examples of this were behind the 2008 meltdown of most financial institutions.) Your authors believe *it is better to be roughly right than precisely wrong*. Further, we agree with Graham about the importance of a margin of safety. While we can rarely buy dollar bills for 50 cents, we generally aren't tempted unless dollars are priced below 80 cents.

PART II

Investing Fundamentals: CAPM and EMH

CHAPTER 6

How Valuation Is Used by Hedge Funds

Value investors, and the long strategies of hedge funds, will screen for companies whose current price is well below their estimate of intrinsic value. The short component of a hedge fund strategy will do the opposite: they will short firms whose market price is well above intrinsic value.

How and Why Events Affect Prices

If a company's value is—optimistically—the present value of all of its future cash flows, then new information that changes expectations about those cash flows will change stock prices.

If most trades occur when the buyer has a different view of the stock's value than the seller, then the receipt of value-relevant news presents an opportunity. If negative news about a company occurs, sellers may wish to unload the stock now in the hope that the buyers who are not yet aware of it will continue to value the stock based on old information that indicates a higher price. Similarly, if buyers believe they know positive news sooner than do sellers, they can buy the stock before sellers upgrade their asking price. So self-interest can drive stock prices up or down out of proportion to the apparent significance of a piece of news, as each trader tries to exploit it before others. A market's efficiency reflects the speed at which this happens.

A study by MacKinlay examined the effects of good and bad news on stock prices, tracing prices for 21 days before and 21 days after an event, where events were characterized as good news, bad news, or no news. Averaging over many companies and their events, bad news generally reduced stock prices by a few percent. Typically the price fell by 2 to 3 percent immediately after the news, then partly recovered in the ensuing days, ending 1 to 2 percent below the price just before the event. The pattern after good news was the mirror image: prices jumped immediately after the event, then partly retraced, ending up 1 to 2 percent 21 days after the event. Interestingly, prices followed a similar, but less pronounced, trajectory before the event: sliding slowly down in the 21 days before the bad news, or creeping slowly up in the 21 days before good news. This again suggests the market is quite efficient, with investors anticipating the news and trading accordingly in advance of the actual event.

Events can be company specific, industry specific, or economy wide. Many "macro" hedge funds specialize in investing based on expected indirect and secondary effects of events. For example, a belief that developed economies will slow might lead a fund to short Chinese manufacturers, on the theory that those firms that export will see slower sales as demand from consumers of developed world declines. As an extension of this idea, an event that negatively affects one industry may help an industry that produces a substitute product: A drought in coffee-producing regions might cause some beverage drinkers to switch to tea, helping tea producers. A hedge fund might short coffee companies and go long in tea companies.

Event studies are discussed at greater length in Chapter 11.

Bio: David Einhorn, Greenlight Capital

Born: 1968

Firm: Greenlight Capital, midtown Manhattan

Founded: 1996

Style: Long/short value–oriented equity.

Annual return: "north of 19 percent," according to Forbes

AUM: $8 billion (2012)

Einhorn's background: He was born in New Jersey and raised mostly in Wisconsin. He graduated from Cornell in 1991 with a bachelor's in Government. He founded Greenlight with $900,000 in his own and family funds. Greenlight's early years, and a deep look into its short of Allied Capital based on Einhorn's suspicions of accounting fraud, are detailed in his book Fooling Some of the People All of the Time, *published in 2008, with a second edition in 2010.*

Significant trades: Major shorts (covered extensively in the media) include Allied Capital in the mid-2000s; Lehmann Brothers in 2007 (18 months before its bankruptcy), and Green Mountain Coffee Roasters in 2011. In April 2013, Einhorn filed a lawsuit against Apple to pressure it to issue dividend-paying preferred stock, to return some of its $100 + billion in cash to shareholders.

Color: Einhorn founded the "Portfolios with Purpose" virtual stock trading contest, with proceeds to charity; and he donates his winnings in the World Series of Poker to charity. In the summer of 2011, Einhorn entered into negotiations to purchase a minority stake in the New York Mets for $200 million, but those talks were suspended by the autumn.

CHAPTER 7

Framework for Investing: The Capital Asset Pricing Model (CAPM)

Although finance and investing have existed as long as there have been markets to connect suppliers of capital (savers) with those who need capital (businesses), the beginnings of a rigorous framework for appraising and designing portfolios did not really come into being until the mid-twentieth century. The Capital Assets Pricing Model (CAPM) is one of the most influential models developed to address this. Merton Miller, Franco Modigliani, and William Sharpe shared a Nobel Prize in Economics in 1990 for their development of the CAPM.

To jump ahead for a moment, one of the core implications of CAPM when combined with the Efficient Markets Hypothesis (EMH), which will be described in the next chapter, is that very few investors can produce sustained returns superior to market averages. Therefore, CAPM and EMH adherents asserted, buying "the market," such as a stock market index, would produce superior results to most other strategies. Burton Malkiel's *A Random Walk Down Wall Street* was the first popular book on *indexing*; first published in 1973, it has now appeared in over a dozen new editions. John Bogle founded Vanguard Funds in the early 1970s to make *index investing* available to retail customers.

Hedge funds are premised on the belief that it is in fact possible to outperform a long-only market indexing strategy. So why spend a chapter on a framework that seems to contradict this? Because CAPM has been hugely influential in the investment community. And because it presents a framework that allows us to break down investing performance into component parts.

An Overview of CAPM

FIgure 7.1 shows daily price movements of a stock, ExxonMobil (ticker symbol XOM) and an index, the S&P 500 (ticker symbol SPX), for about 1 year from late 2011 to late 2012.

You can see that prices of these two assets *mostly* move in tandem. But there are periods where one moves by more, or less, than the other. This suggests two things:

- There appears to be a strong relationship (positive correlation) between XOM and SPX—that is, most events seem to affect both assets in the same general way.
- Changes in XOM do not appear (for the most part) to be quite as pronounced as changes in SPX.

Clearly, relative price movements for a given stock—in this case XOM—compared to the overall market—captured in the S&P 500 index, SPX—deserve attention. But there may also be a systematic difference in a stock's returns, aside from the portion of its returns that seem to relate to broader market movements. That is the core of CAPM: distinguishing

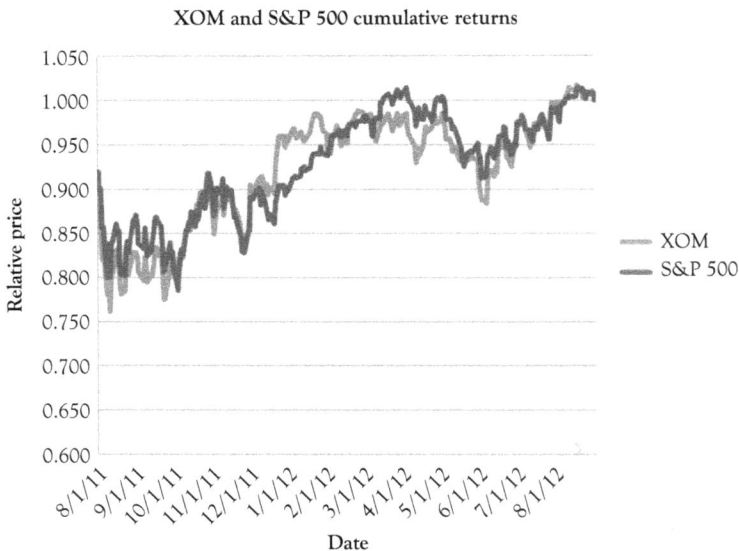

Figure 7.1 Daily price movements for XOM and SPX

between stock returns that derive from broad market movements and those that do not.

The ABCs of CAPM: Alphas, Betas, and Correlations

Figure 7.2 shows the price *changes* (i.e., the daily returns in percent) in XOM and SPX. In many instances, the two series are indistinguishable, a sign that whatever affects the overall market (SPX) is also affecting ExxonMobil (XOM). Recall that returns are simply

$$[(\text{Price at time } t/\text{Price at time } t - 1) - 1].$$

The most basic measure of the relationship between movements in XOM's price and SPX is *correlation*. In a simple form, a correlation coefficient measures the frequency with which prices of two assets move in the same direction. Correlation coefficients can be as follows:

- −1.0—a perfect negative relationship. Whenever the S&P rises, XOM falls, and vice versa.
- 0—no visible relationship.
- +1.0—a perfect positive relationship. Whenever the S&P rises, XOM rises, and vice versa.

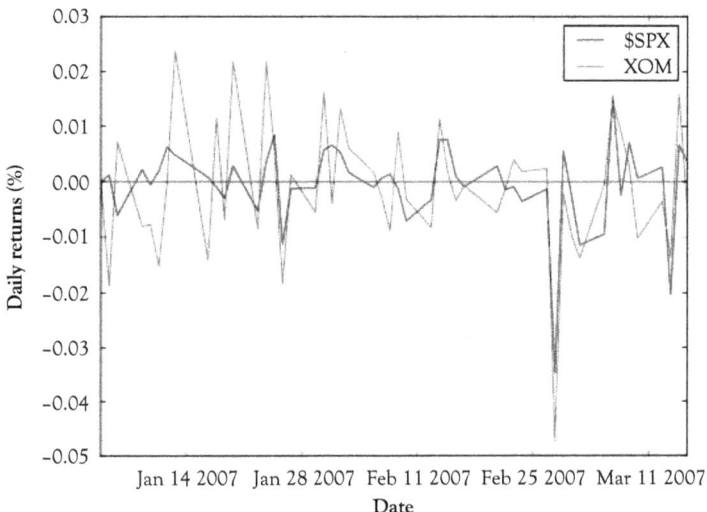

Figure 7.2 Daily percentage change in price for SPX and XOM

Correlations among financial instruments will be essential elements of portfolio construction, discussed in a later chapter. In general, combining assets with low or negative correlations to each other—that is, correlation coefficients that are near zero, or even negative—dampens a portfolio's volatility (i.e., lowers risk).

The essence of CAPM is illustrated in Figure 7.3. This is a scatter plot of XOM's daily returns versus those of SPX. Each dot represents one day of data—the horizontal location indicates the change in SPX, while the vertical location is the change in XOM. This pattern of a generally upward-sloping oval-shaped scatter is very common: On days when the overall market is driven upward (i.e., when there are more buyers than sellers), the same is true of XOM. This implies the correlation coefficient is positive (between 0 and 1). If XOM benefitted from events that hurt the overall market (or vice versa), the general shape of the scatter would be downward, and the SPX and XOM correlation coefficient would be negative (between –1 and 0).

As shown in Figure 7.3, we can fit a regression line through this scatter to find the linear equation that best captures its pattern. All linear equations have the general form $Y = b \times X + a$; in this example:

$$\text{Return (XOM)} = \text{beta} \times \text{Return (SPX)} + \text{alpha}$$

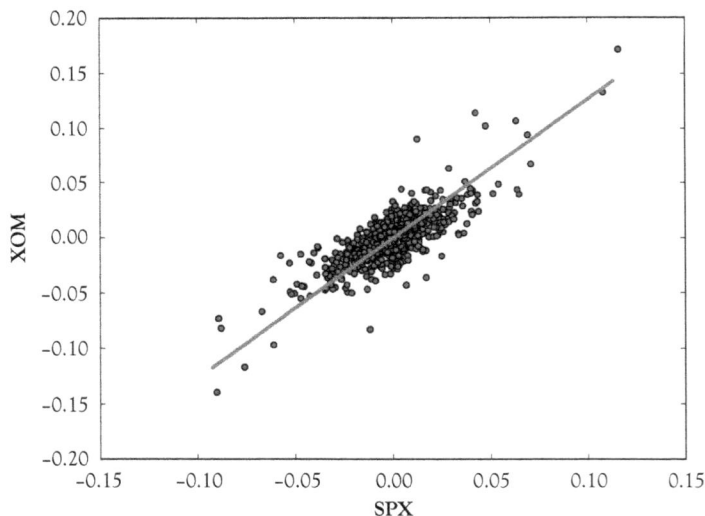

Figure 7.3 Scatter graph of XOM return versus market return, with regression line

where alpha is the *Y*-intercept of the regression line, and beta is its slope.

We can interpret these ABCs—alphas, betas, and correlations—as follows:

- *Alpha* is the systematic difference in performance (return) of a stock over and above the market. Positive alpha could come from superior management, production technology, or product design; or from having a dominant position in the company's market that provides it pricing power (the ability to raise prices without losing many customers). Alpha is the intercept of the regression line in Figure 4.3. Since collectively all stocks cannot beat the market because together they *are* the market, alpha is assumed to be zero on average. (Any stock with positive alphas is counterbalanced by other stocks with negative alphas.)

- *Beta* represents the stock's price volatility relative to the overall market. Simply put, a stock with a beta of, say, 1.5 will rise on average 1.5 times as much, and fall 1.5 times as much, as the overall market, in percentage terms. Small, speculative companies usually have betas well above 1.0, while large companies with very stable earnings usually have betas well under 1.0. XOM's beta is 0.77; it isn't surprising that a large company whose fortunes are so intertwined with other companies (through oil supplier relationships) would see its stock move almost as much as the overall market. The market's beta is by definition 1.0. Beta is the slope of the regression line as shown in Figure 7.3. You can find a stock's beta on many investing websites, such as Google Finance or Yahoo Finance.

- *Correlation coefficients* capture the "tightness" of the scatter around the regression line, which summarizes the pattern in that scatter. The higher (closer to 1.0) the correlation between XOM and SPX, the more that XOM's price movements are explained by movements in SPX. Said differently, a high correlation coefficient suggests that events that affect prices in the overall market have similar effects on the price of XOM.

Implications of CAPM

A fund manager can derive return from beta and alpha: When returns are based primarily on an upward general market we call this *buying beta*. On the other hand, returns resulting from investment skill are known as *seeking alpha*. As noted earlier, extensive study of the mutual fund industry finds little evidence of persistent alpha among fund managers.

So CAPM allows the most basic disaggregation of an investment's performance into two parts: based on market return (which could be achieved simply by buying an index)—beta; and based on company-specific factors—alpha. Since there are extremely inexpensive ways to guarantee a beta of 1.0 by buying index funds or ETFs, outperforming the market entails investing in stocks more volatile than the index (buying beta), or finding stocks that systematically outperform (buying alpha). Buying beta means, by definition, buying increased risk, since high beta stocks not only rise faster than the index on "up" days, but also fall farther on "down" days. Buying alpha is the oft-sought, but rarely achieved goal.

Basic Hedge Fund Strategies in the CAPM Framework

Hedge funds are so called because the first hedge fund, Albert Winslow Jones' fund formed in 1949, strove for absolute positive returns through hedging—making contrary bets that would pay off if their main bet failed. These hedges would at a minimum reduce losses, and in the best case could produce absolute positive returns (i.e., returns above zero even if the general market direction was downward). In exchange, these hedges posed a drag on returns when the market headed upward.

In CAPM terms, a hedge works as follows. (We will retain the XOM and SPX example from the previous figures.)

A portfolio's return is the weighted average of the returns of its constituent assets. (Portfolio construction will be treated at length in later chapters.) So if an investor holds a portfolio that constitutes a long position in XOM for 60 percent of its holdings and in SPY (SPY is a publicly traded ETF that tracks SPX) for 40 percent, the portfolio's return would be calculated as follows:

XOM weight: 60 percent; XOM return: 8 percent

SPY weight: 40 percent; SPY return: 10 percent

Portfolio return: 60% × 8% + 40% × 10% = 4.8% + 4% = 8.8%.

    (XOM)   (SPY)   (Portfolio)

As you would expect, the portfolio's return falls between that of its two constituents, shaded toward XOM, which has a larger share of the overall portfolio.

In CAPM terms, a portfolio's return is likewise an amalgam of the returns on each stock within it:

return (portfolio) = weight (XOM) × return (XOM) + weight (SPY) × return (SPY), where each stock's return is as follows:

return (XOM) = beta (XOM) × return (market) + alpha (XOM)

and

return (SPY) = beta (SPY) × return (market) + alpha (SPY)

Note: We assume beta for SPY is 1.0 and that SPY's alpha is 0 because its performance is equivalent to the market's.

Let's move on now to a hedge example: Assume that the investor has some reason to believe that Exxon will experience positive developments and will rise faster than the overall market. A long-only investor would simply buy XOM. If it performs as expected, the investor will do well; however, if the market drops substantially, XOM will drop with it and he will lose money.

To hedge against this possibility—that XOM may decline because the overall market declines—when a hedge fund buys a long position in XOM, it can short the SPX. Accordingly, suppose the manager takes a 50 percent positive position in XOM, and a negative 50 percent position in SPY: The portfolio return is the weighted average of the two positions:

0.5 × [beta (XOM) × return (market) + alpha (XOM)] +

−0.5 × [beta (SPY) × return (market) + alpha (SPY)]

The portfolio weight for SPY has a negative sign because the fund is shorting the SPX. Again note that the alpha for SPY—the market—is by definition 0.

If the investor's forecast is incorrect and XOM falls (not rises as he expected), the tumble may be because of a general fall in the market, in which case his short would make money that would at least partly compensate for his loss in the long XOM position. At the same time, if his forecast is correct and both XOM and the overall market rise, his XOM gains will be at least partly offset (dragged down) by his losses on the short SPX position.

Note that this portfolio (50 percent XOM, −50 percent SPY) is dollar balanced, meaning that there is an equivalent investment on the long side as on the short side. But the portfolio is not beta balanced. The two positions do not quite cancel each other out—the portfolio will still be skewed long or short by the respective alphas and betas of its two positions. In this instance, it's because XOM's beta (0.77) is lower than SPY's (1.0). If the market goes up the portfolio will only be net long if XOM's alpha is sufficiently greater than the market's to counteract the 0.23 difference in betas (1.0 − 0.77). However, if the betas of the two issues were very close, the positive return would be 0.5 × the long position's alpha (in this case, XOM's).

Most hedge funds seek beta-balanced portfolios so that they are precisely protected against market-wide moves. That means, essentially

$$Sum(beta\_i * w\_i) = 0, \text{ and}$$
$$Sum(|w\_i|) = 1.0$$

where beta_i is the beta for stock I, and w_i is its weight in the portfolio. In this case, because XOM's beta is 0.77, we must hold a larger portion of XOM to offset its lower beta. A beta-balanced portfolio of these two issues would contain 56 percent XOM, and −44 percent in SPY. (We leave the algebra as an exercise.)

Such excess returns are quite small, which is why hedge funds need to trade in very large volumes, and often use leverage (borrowing) to expand the magnitude of their trades. Many financial institutions like hedge funds leverage 20 or 30 times their invested capital. Leverage magnifies both gains *and* losses. This is why high degrees of leverage are often combined with hedged (long/short) strategies.

CHAPTER 8

The Efficient Market Hypothesis (EMH)—Its Three Versions

Another extremely influential element of finance theory is the idea that most asset markets are highly *efficient*. In this context, *efficiency* means that information that can affect prices travels quickly throughout a market and that their prices are affected accordingly. Recall that arbitrage opportunities exist when a buyer and a seller have differing views of the true price of a stock—perhaps because of differences in information available. The more efficient a market, the more that relevant information is equally available to all market participants. Many disclosure requirements in law and regulation aim to improve the efficiency of the market. Likewise, prohibitions on insider trading are intended to make it difficult for those company insiders to exploit their information advantage. (Most criminal cases involving hedge fund personnel have been related to insider trading.)

What Makes Markets Efficient?

An indirect measure of market efficiency is the speed with which a stock's price adjusts to company-relevant information. Why would this occur? Let's consider a few examples:

1. Say, for example, that a mining company reports that the results of test borings of a new mine yielded less gold per ton than expected. Interested investors might conclude that the company's profits would be depressed because the cost to generate an ounce of gold in the future will be higher than expected.

2. Lower than expected earnings could have a double effect: It will reduce the company's stock price for a given price to earnings (P/E) ratio; and the reduced prospects might lower the stock's P/E. Investors who follow the stock closely will rush to unload their shares before (they hope) others realize that the stock has become less valuable. In this way, investor self-interest will cause new information to be reflected in stock prices quite quickly.

Asset markets undoubtedly vary in their efficiency. Those with very high trading volumes and significant transparency (i.e., wide disclosure of relevant information), such as the NYSE, are at the high end of the efficiency spectrum. Illiquid, niche markets with poor information transmission, such as a "frontier" stock market in an emerging economy, will be much less efficient.

Market efficiency is crucial to determining whether active investment management, such as by hedge funds, is cost-effective. In highly efficient markets, several investment managers may be competing to profit from arbitrage opportunities that those opportunities are "arbitraged away" almost instantaneously.

Three Versions of the EMH

Eugene Fama first postulated the EMH in the mid-1960s. As elaborated by others, it has now been posed in three different, increasingly rigorous versions:

1. *Weak form*: Future asset prices *cannot* be predicted using historical price and volume data. Such information is widely available from the business press and on investing websites such as Google Finance or Yahoo Finance.
2. *Semi-strong form*: Asset prices adjust immediately to all publicly available information, including that which reflects the company's fundamentals like financial disclosures.
3. *Strong form*: Asset prices adjust immediately to reflect all relevant information, including that available to insiders.

Which form of the EMH best approximates real conditions will fundamentally affect which investing strategies can succeed.

If the *weak form* of the EMH is correct, technical analysis (using only historical price and volume data) cannot succeed, but investors who can develop other relevant information (such as independent fundamental estimates of intrinsic value) can have and exploit an information advantage.

If the *semi-strong form* is correct, technical analysis and fundamental analysis cannot work: Value investors are wasting their time—value arbitrage opportunities don't exist, because they have been already arbitraged away.

If the *strong form* is correct, even those who trade on inside information cannot succeed: They are risking jail to little gain.

Debates over the EMH

Most academic studies have supported the validity of some version of the EMH. A good layman's summary is Burton Malkiel's *A Random Walk Down Wall Street*. As noted earlier, it is likely that different versions apply in different markets. The strongest versions apply in the largest, most transparent, most liquid markets such as for U.S. large cap stocks. In these markets, numerous studies have demonstrated that very few managers persistently outperform market indexes—even fewer than would be expected by mere chance.

A casual reader might conclude that if the EMH applies, then hedge funds or any active management approach could not succeed, and that they incur expenses with no sustained benefit. As noted earlier, this supposition seems reasonable for most managers, based on extensive empirical research by economic and finance academics. But such reasoning may be overdone. Active managers may be precisely the agents who make a market efficient! They have incentive to identify any possible opportunity to arbitrage. Because their competitors seek similar opportunities, they have reason to act on those they identify as quickly as possible. So hedge funds may contribute to the existence of efficient markets, rather than being made unnecessary by them. While high hedge fund fees may offer dubious value to clients, they may provide a more general service by incentivizing greater market efficiency.

CHAPTER 9

The Fundamental Law
of Active Portfolio
Management

*Wide diversification is only required when investors do not under-
stand what they are doing.*

—Warren Buffett

Buffett's quote seems to contradict quantitative investment approaches:
Quant funds often diversify across hundreds or thousands of positions.
Do quant funds know what they are doing?

You already know Warren Buffett is an effective fund manager, perhaps
the best ever (see Figure 9.1). What might we learn from his investing style?
We can learn a lot of course, but let's focus here on his allocation strategy:
How does he apportion Berkshire Hathaway's (BRK-A and BRK-B) assets
across the various equities they hold? (Figure 9.1).

Buffett invests strongly in a small number of companies: As of Septem-
ber 2010, 54 percent of BRK-A's holdings were in just three stocks: Coca
Cola (KO), American Express (AXP), and Wells Fargo (WFC). Ninety
percent of their holdings were in just 12 stocks. Let's compare Buffett's allocation with Renaissance Technologies' Medallion Fund. Renaissance Technologies (RenTec) is perhaps the most successful quantitative hedge fund
management firm, with consistent annual returns of 35 percent or more
for their Medallion Fund each year. In contrast to BRK, RenTec's portfolio
is distributed more or less uniformly across hundreds of positions.

So we have two very different but successful allocation strategies. They
are at either end of a spectrum: One with just a few holdings (BRK-A) and
another with hundreds (RenTec). You may be interested to learn about an
investment theory that explains how they can both be successful.

Figure 9.1 *Performance of Berkshire Hathaway*
Source: Yahoo.com

Relating Performance, Skill, and Breadth

In the 1980s, Richard Grinold introduced what he calls the Fundamental Law of Active Portfolio Management. It is described nicely in his book with Ronald Kahn, *Active Portfolio Management*. For the moment we will offer a simplified version of this law. We paraphrase it as follows:

$$performance = skill * \sqrt{breadth}$$

Skill is a measure of how well a manager transforms information about an equity into an accurate prediction of future return, and *breadth* represents the number of investment decisions (trades) the manager makes each year. This law suggests that as a manager's skill increases, returns increase. That is not surprising. What is interesting and perhaps surprising is that to double performance at the same level of skill, a manager must find *four times* as many opportunities to trade.

The law also implies that Buffett could improve his performance significantly by expanding his portfolio. Why doesn't he do that? We can only speculate, but it is likely because his skill does not scale. Not only that, he is probably aware of the diminishing returns suggested by the Fundamental Law: If he worked twice as hard by looking at more companies, returns would only improve by 41 percent. Buffett spends a great deal of time understanding a small number of companies deeply. His attention and depth enables him to make accurate predictions for the companies he thinks about. But he can't apply this depth of attention to all of the 4,000 equities traded on the NYSE.

On the other hand, RenTec's predictive power is not as strong as Buffett's, but it is scalable. They use computerized techniques to assess thousands of equities in a more shallow way. But they do it rapidly, perhaps hundreds of times a second. The accuracy of each of their predictions is not as high as Buffett's, but because they are able to apply a modest level of skill to so many equities their breadth substantially outpaces his.

Breadth as Diversification

There are two ways to increase the breadth of a portfolio: We can choose to hold more equities at once, or we can turn over those assets more frequently. The first approach is more suitable for a conventional managed portfolio approach to investing, while the second relates more to an active trading strategy. In this section, we'll take a look at the managed portfolio.

You've heard the cliché "Don't put all your eggs in one basket." If you run into a negative surprise regarding that basket, you will be glad that all your eggs are not there. By the same token, if the basket surprises you positively, you will regret having spread your bets around.

Modern portfolio theory distinguishes between two broad categories of risk:

- *Systematic risk* is that risk undertaken by exposure to any asset in the asset class. You may invest in the bluest blue chip stock, but it too will take a beating if the entire market falls.
- *Specific risk* is the risk associated with a particular asset. An oil company's stock price may suffer if a new oil field fails to produce as expected—regardless of what else is occurring in the stock market.

Diversification mutes specific risk. Research has shown that the volatility, or standard deviation of returns, of a portfolio of stocks declines as more individual stocks are included in the portfolio. Accordingly, some investment advisors counsel limiting any single position to no more than 5 percent of a total portfolio. (Some recommend even lower percentages.) But the benefit decelerates as the portfolio becomes too diverse. Experts argue that diversification beyond 20 to 40 separate issues provides little additional risk reduction.

There is a trade-off, however. The more breadth in an investor's port-folio, the less expertise they can apply to each of its contents. Since alpha is assumed to stem from research and knowledge—that is, from invest-ment-specific information—the broader the portfolio, the less alpha can be generated.

Breadth as More Frequent Trading

Another approach to adding breadth to a portfolio or strategy is through more trading opportunities. We will illustrate that idea here using a sim-ple example of an even money bet: coin flipping.

Assume you have been given a coin and invited to wager on the result of a series of coin flips. Each flip requires you to bet a fixed amount, which you choose; say $1 at the start. If the coin lands on the side you predict, you receive a second dollar: a 100 percent return. If it lands on the other side, you lose your bet: a –100 percent return. If the coin was *fair* (i.e., it could fall on either side with an equal 50 percent probability), then the expected return of any one-dollar bet would be zero, regardless of how many times you bet:

$$\text{Expected return for each flip: } = \text{Prob (heads)} \times \text{Reward (heads)}$$
$$+ \text{ Prob (tails)} \times \text{Reward (tails)}$$
$$= 0.50 \times \$1 + 0.50 \times (-\$1) = 0$$

Therefore, the total expected return would be zero regardless of the num-ber of flips for one dollar each.

But say your coin wasn't fair—it had a small bias toward one side, say heads. Let that small bias reflect skill. Assume the bias creates a 51 percent probability of heads and a 49 percent probability of tails. Clearly your expected return for each flip will now be positive:

$$\text{Expected return for each flip: } 0.51 \times \$1 + 0.49 \times (-\$1)$$
$$= 0.51 - (-.49) = 0.02 \text{ (two cents)}$$

Clearly this is a bet you wish to take. The question is, for how much each flip? Say you have $1,000 to bet. Should you bet it all on a single $1,000 flip, or flip 1,000 times for 1,000 individual one dollar bets? This is analo-gous to the question: How diverse should your portfolio be?

The expected return is the same whether you make one bet of $1,000 or 1,000 bets of $1:

0.02 × 1,000   = $20;
(Exp return per bet) × (# of bets) = (Exp return for all bets)

or

$20 × 1   = $20
(Exp return per bet) × (# of bets)   = (Exp return for all bets)

The expected return is the same for each situation, but the risk is very different.

First, for the single bet option, there is a 49 percent chance that you will lose your entire $1,000 stake. For the multiple bet option, the probability of a total loss—the coin coming up tails each of 1,000 times—is $0.49 \wedge 1000$, which is infinitesimal (too small to be displayed on our spreadsheet, even to 23 significant digits). So, for this measure, risk is substantially lower for the 1000-bet scenario.

But we can also use standard deviation—a measure of the range of plausible returns—as a measure of risk. For a single $1,000 bet, the standard deviation is $31.62. For the 1,000 $1 bets, the standard deviation is $1. So for this measure, we also see significantly lower the risk for the 1000- bet case. In finance, we often compare strategies in terms of risk-adjusted return, which is to say return divided by the risk. So the return to risk ratios of the two options are as follows:

Single $1,000 bet: $20 reward/$31.62 risk (standard deviation) = 0.6325
One thousand $1 bets: $20 reward/$1 risk = 20.0

This return to risk ratio is similar to the Sharpe ratio. But it is not based on excess return—it doesn't explicitly deduct a no-risk return from our expected return. But if the risk-free return is zero—if the only way to earn a return is by betting on coin flips—then this is essentially the Sharpe ratio. This specific version is called the *information ratio*, discussed later in this chapter.

The "diverse" option where we are able to flip the coin more times has a reward to risk ratio more than 30 times that of the concentrated option!

A Few Definitions

We will soon present the fundamental law in full. But we must first introduce some terminology. The Fundamental Law relates overall portfolio performance to investor skill and breadth (or diversification). In our coin flipping example, breadth is reflected in the number of flips, while for investing, it relates to the number of investment opportunities.

To fully explain the fundamental law, we need to introduce two new terms. These are, frankly, not well labeled. But their names have become commonly used, so we are stuck with them.

Information Ratio

A key measure of performance used in quantitative portfolio management is the *information ratio (IR)*. IR is similar to the Sharpe ratio; it adjusts return for risk, by dividing them:

IR = excess return per period/(standard deviation of excess return per period)

We must be more specific now by what we mean by "excess return." In particular, we seek to measure return that is due to the investor's skill rather than return that is due to the market. Recall that the CAPM separates market return from stock-specific return:

$$\text{return (stock } i) = \text{beta } (i) \times \text{return (market)} + \text{alpha } (i)$$

The alpha component is sometimes called the "residual." It reflects the component of price movement that cannot be attributed to the market overall. It is sometimes attributed to the skill of the investor for having selected the stock. Because returns vary daily, the aforementioned terms are usually averages (means) of a series of daily returns. Their variation, or risk, is captured by their standard deviations. You can think of the total return as having two risk components:

- Market risk, captured by the standard deviation of [beta × return (market)].
- Investor-specific or "skill" risk, captured by the standard deviation of alpha.

Hedging investing strategies seek to minimize or eliminate the market risk, leaving a clear field to exploit the investor's alpha. A summary measure of skill is the information ratio of an investor's alpha, or:

$$IR\ (alpha) = Mean\ (alpha)/Standard\ deviation\ (alpha).$$

This adjusts the average excess return the investor earns by the risk he runs.

Information Coefficient

A manager's *information coefficient* (IC) is the correlation of a manager's predictions about asset prices with their actual future prices. A perfect predictor would have an IC of 1.0; a perfectly wrong predictor would have an IC of -1.0. IC captures the quality of the information a manager uses in forecasting prices.

Breadth

The breadth (BR) of a portfolio or management strategy is simply the number of trading opportunities presented over time.

The Fundamental Law in Full

Grinold's Fundamental Law of Active Portfolio Management relates IR to IC and breadth as follows:

$$IR = IC * \sqrt{breadth}$$

Implications of the Fundamental Law

An increment of added skill, reflected in the information coefficient, has a greater reflect on risk-adjusted return (the information ratio) than does an equal increment in portfolio breadth. This is because the portfolio breadth affects the IR as a square root, whereas IC affects IR proportionally. So for an investor like Buffett, whose IC is probably among the highest on the planet, he is absolutely correct—for him—to disparage diversification.

As was mentioned earlier, expanding a portfolio's breadth often means expanding beyond what Buffett calls the investor's "circle of competence." That is why, for example, he eschewed technology businesses during the dot com era. In other words, there may be a physical trade-off between breadth and IC. For both these reasons it is rational to seek a higher IC rather than increased portfolio diversity—*if* you can actually improve your IC.

Bio: Jim Simons, Renaissance Technologies

Born: 1938, raised in Brookline, Massachusetts

Firm: Renaissance Technologies (RenTec). Flagship fund: Medallion Fund

Founded: 1982

Annual return: 39 percent, 1989 to 2006

AUM: $20 billion (2010)

Style: Quantitative all-asset trend-following, specializing in commodities

Simons background: B.S. in Math, MIT; PhD in Math, UC Berkeley. Mathematician and code-breaker at the Institute for Defense Analysis (IDA); winner of the highest prize in geometry. Fired from IDA for opposition to the Vietnam War, Simons rode from Boston to Bogota, Columbia, on a motor scooter. He then launched a factory in Colombia. Successfully traded commodities during the high-inflation, high-volatility late 1970s, collecting a team of applied mathematicians who used the principles of cryptography to "decode" commodity price patterns.

Differentiation: RenTec employs many scientists and mathematicians without financial backgrounds, believing that they can examine financial data without preconceptions. "Simons' team took their experience with code-breaking algorithms and used it to look for ghostly patterns in market data. Economists could not compete in the same league, because they lacked the specialized math to do so." (from More Money Than God*)*

PART III

Market Simulation and Portfolio Construction

CHAPTER 10

Modern Portfolio Theory: The Efficient Frontier and Portfolio Optimization

Investors want the best possible return for a given amount of risk. In other words, they want to maximize *risk-adjusted* returns. Portfolio design is about the creation of a collection of assets whose combined risk level may be lower than that for any individual component. This apparent magic was first formalized by Harry Markowitz in the 1950s. He shared a Nobel Prize for this work, and his original ideas have been extended by other academics. These ideas are known collectively as modern portfolio theory (MPT). In this chapter we will use a stylized example to make the core elements of MPT clear (Figure 10.1).

Risk and Return, Again

Assume your portfolio can be composed of a range of specific assets, such as company stocks or individual bonds. Each of these can be classified in risk and return space based on your expectations for each. Expectations may be based on a forecast, or on past experience (implicitly assuming that the asset's future behavior will resemble its past behavior). Figure 10.2 illustrates a typical scatter plot for a range of assets. Note that individual stocks' returns and risks seem to be randomly distributed, but with an upward bias: Generally, it isn't possible to enhance return without accepting more risk. Looking at it another way, in an efficient market, investors will price low risk and high return assets highly in the first place, thereby depressing future returns. Only volatile (risky) assets will be priced low and produce superior returns. This *risk and return trade-off* is one of the fundamental assumptions in modern finance.

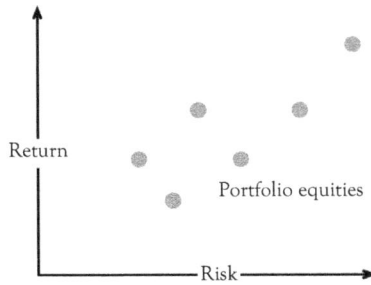

Figure 10.1 Risk and returns for asset classes

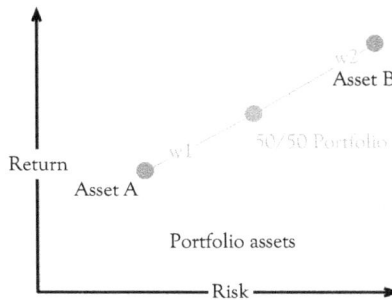

Figure 10.2 Risk and returns for two pure asset classes and one 50/50 portfolio

Once assets are selected (e.g., which stocks to buy) a key decision in the construction of a portfolio is to select the proportions we use of each asset, called portfolio weights or allocations. The *efficient frontier* connects the assets that lie generally above and to the left of all other assets on the scatter plot. If 100 percent of our portfolio is in Asset A, its risk and return are those of point A in Figure 10.2. A 50/50 mix of Assets A and B will usually produce risk and return about halfway between points A and B. In principle, it seems we should be able to extrapolate this to a portfolio with any number of assets: We would expect its risk and return to fall roughly in the center of the included points (assets included in the portfolio), closer to the heaviest-weighted assets. An example is Figure 10.3. But this need not be the case: The right combination of assets can reduce risk at little cost in return. This apparent magic is known as portfolio construction, specifically portfolio optimization.

To explain this magic entails a brief digression into the profound importance of correlations in a portfolio.

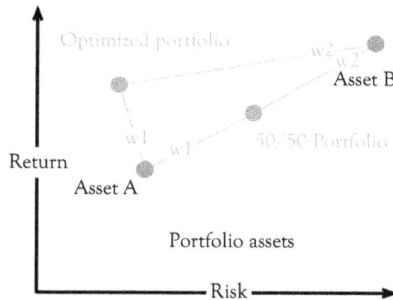

Figure 10.3 Risk and returns for mixed and optimized portfolios

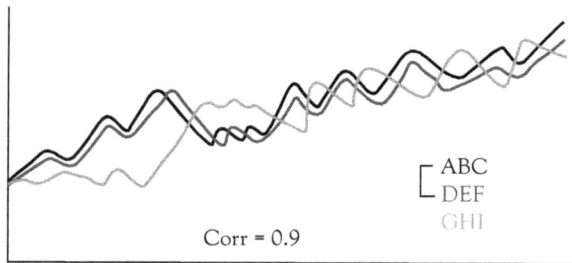

Figure 10.4 Price history of stocks ABC, DEF, and GHI

Why Low Correlation Is Prized

Figure 10.4 shows the price history of three stocks, with tickers ABC, DEF, and GHI. Each achieves about the same return over the period, and appears to have similar volatility (standard deviation), based on the graph alone. You can see that ABC and DEF move virtually in tandem, so events appear to affect them similarly. These two stocks have a very high positive correlation (say, 0.9). Buying both does not really diversify your portfolio. In contrast, GHI seems to move opposite to ABC and DEF: it rises when they fall, and vice versa. GHI appears to be highly *negatively correlated* with ABC and DEF (say, –0.9).

Creating a portfolio combining GHI for 50 percent with each of ABC (25 percent) and DEF (25 percent) will produce Figure 10.5, the portfolio's price history over the same period. Its total return will be the weighted average of the returns of the three stocks, as expected. But what is surprising is that *the portfolio's volatility is far less than any of its components.*

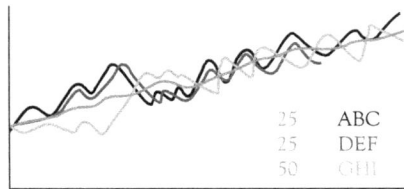

Figure 10.5 Price history of portfolio of stocks ABC (25 percent), DEF (25 percent), and GHI (50 percent)

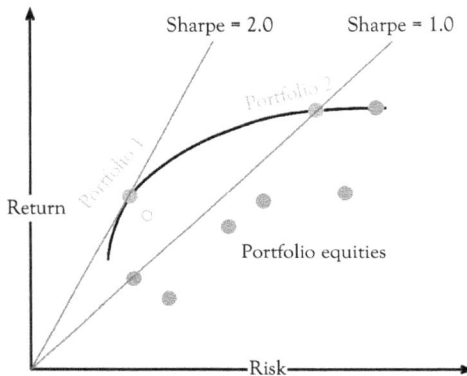

Figure 10.6 Scatter plot of asset risks and returns

The reason for this is that the portfolio combines assets that are negatively correlated. This dampens the oscillations in return and produces much less volatility than any of the three stocks achieve by themselves.

Figure 10.6 now returns us to the scatter plot of portfolio components in terms of risk and return, but with two important additions:

- Since our measure of risk-adjusted return, the Sharpe ratio, is the ratio of the vertical (return) divided by the horizontal (risk) in Figure 10.6, the slope of a ray from the origin outward that passes through a portfolio's location is that portfolio's Sharpe ratio. The point on the efficient frontier that intersects with the steepest-sloped ray has the highest Share ratio—it delivers the most return per unit of risk.

- Combining assets with negative correlations but similar returns can lower risk without sacrificing return. In practice, few assets are negatively correlated, so we will have to settle for low positive correlations. But the same principle applies, if not as strongly.

Assume for the moment that Portfolio 1 in Figure 10.6 is our designed portfolio, found by combining several weakly correlated asset choices. You can see that it is above and to the left of most assets in the scatter plot. It will have the highest Sharpe ratio (the steepest-sloped ray from the origin). This is the goal of portfolio optimization: to design the combination of assets that produces the lowest risk for a specified target return.

Optimization Basics

Optimization means identifying the best choice among a number of options. In the context of a portfolio, this means choosing what fraction of the portfolio should comprise each of the available assets. Assets could be specific issues such as individual companies' common stock, or asset classes such as large cap, midcap, small cap, and microcap equities; short-, intermediate-, or long-term bonds; residential, commercial, or industrial real estate, and so forth—whatever asset class trades on a major exchange.

Most optimization problems have common components. They are listed here, with explanation specific to portfolio optimization.

1. *Decision variables*: Proportion of portfolio devoted to each asset (portfolio weights).
2. *Objective function*: Goal you wish to maximize or minimize. Commonly, portfolio optimizers minimize risk, but they could maximize total portfolio return. The objective function has a coefficient on each portfolio element that reflects that element's contribution to the goal. For an investment portfolio, such coefficients would be each asset's return.
3. *Constraints*: Limits you impose on the set the optimizer should consider. If the objective function was to minimize risk, one constraint might be to achieve a total return equal or above a threshold amount.

You may also set minimum and maximum weights on some elements of the portfolio, such as holding no more than 10 percent in bonds rated below investment grade; or no more than 5 percent in any single issue. One definitional constraint is that the sum of all weights in a long-only portfolio cannot exceed 100 percent.

4. *A search procedure*: The optimization algorithm uses some procedure to efficiently search for the best combination of decision variables. In some cases, it may be brute force—trying one combination after another. Generally, it uses some efficient or semiefficient procedure. For example, if the function being maximized is convex, trying alternatives an increment above and below the last trial will determine which weights should be increased and which decreased. Some optimization problems have very efficient solutions; for example, any function for which there is a calculable derivative (remember your high school calculus) will have an immediately identifiable optimum. Similarly, for linear programming problems (optimization problems in which the objective and constraints can be expressed as linear functions), optimal solutions will always be corner solutions, so it is only necessary to compute the objective value in corners (intersections between constraints). Binary search algorithms and similar procedures likewise speed up the process of seeking an optimum.

A publicly available optimizer is available as part of QSTK in the public domain, thanks to the efforts of UCLA. You will find it at http://wiki.quantsoftware.org/index.php?title=QSTK_Tutorial_8. Microsoft Excel also includes a simple optimizer within its macros.

Portfolio Optimization and the Efficient Frontier

Figure 10.7 repeats Figure 10.6 from before, with small additions. You can see that the most desirable portfolios will be located in the upper-left portion of the scatter plot. The point (combination of assets) that intersects with the steepest ray emanating from the origin (Sharpe ratio) will maximize the ratio of return divided by risk. In this figure, two straight lines have been drawn, a horizontal line indicating the target return, and

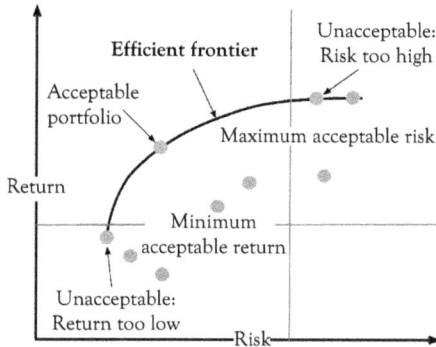

Figure 10.7 *The lowest risk portfolios for each level of return lie along a line called the efficient frontier*

a vertical line indicating the minimum risk portfolio discovered by an optimizer that provides that return.

For each level of target return, there is a set of weights that provides the lowest-risk portfolio for that return. If we chart all these possible portfolios, by optimizing for each target return they form a curve called the *efficient frontier*. Note that the efficient frontier provides lower-risk portfolios (further left) than individual assets with similar returns.

A Dynamic Process

You can see that the optimal portfolio weights for any asset will be greatly affected by its expected return, and its correlation with other assets that are candidates for the portfolio. *These are not stable values.* Returns are cyclical: When an asset becomes popular, buyers bid up its price, which reduces future returns. Correlations can change: If a global event affects two apparently unrelated assets, uncorrelated assets can suddenly become highly correlated. This is common in a market crisis; A Wall Street joke is "in a market meltdown, nothing rises except correlations." When investors feared Depression conditions in the fall of 2008, they rushed to liquidate risky assets—of all types—to move into cash and Treasuries. Bonds and stocks, which are usually relatively uncorrelated, were suddenly highly correlated. So portfolios need to be optimized on a recurring basis.

No Panacea

While optimization can reduce some of the guesswork of portfolio construction, its apparent rigor and scientific basis can be seductive. Any model-based construction suffers from the following limitations:

- *Outputs are only as good as inputs.* Asset allocations depend on forecast returns, and forecasts can be noisy and erroneous. Return data may have biases and errors, such as the survivorship bias in hedge fund returns mentioned later. Quantitative outputs can appear overly rigorous if they are based on flawed inputs.
- *Standard deviation of return is not the only measure of risk.* Other metrics that focus mainly or exclusively on downside deviations in asset returns, such as the Sortino ratio or downside capture, may better reflect what risk means to you.
- *Beware tail risk.* Many hedge fund blowups, such as LTCM's in the summer of 1998 (described in the case study later), occurred because managers underestimated the likelihood of extreme negative events. Portfolios that were designed based on only a few decades of data omitted "black swan" events that last occurred before the data series began. In addition, it is arguable that tails are getting fatter—extreme events are occurring more frequently, and with wider consequences as assets become more closely correlated. In essence, risk was misestimated.

The upshot is that, as with any quantitative decision support tool, it is only a tool, not an oracle.

Bio: Ray Dalio, Bridgewater

Born: 1950

Firm: Bridgewater Associates, Westport, Connecticut

Founded: 1975

Style: Global macro

How it differentiates: (1) Intensive research, (2) exceptional transparency with clients and (3) corporate culture places strong emphasis on introspection and self-criticism—almost cultlike.

Annual return: 18 percent, *since 1991*

Assets under management (AUM): $145 billion (March 2013)

Dalio's background: Ray Dalio grew up in a middle-class family on Long Island, a self-proclaimed "below average" student. He became interested in investing as a preteen golf caddy. It was the early 1960s and the stock market was first emerging from a generation-long slumber following the 1929 Crash and the Great Depression. After college, Dalio went to the Harvard Business School for his MBA, graduating in 1973. He worked as a commodities trader only briefly before being fired for insubordination, leaving to found Bridgewater in 1975. The firm was originally a contract research shop, which moved into money management in the early 1990s. Bridgewater's culture is unique in its emphasis on self-criticism and other principles at the core of Dalio's philosophy.

Colorful quotes (from Dalio's self-published book, Principles*):*

"The consensus is often wrong, so I have to be an independent thinker. To make any money, you have to be right when they're wrong."

"I believe that you can probably get what you want out of life if you can suspend your ego and take a no-excuses approach to achieving your goals with open-mindedness, determination, and courage, especially of you rely on the help of people who are strong in areas where you are weak."

"Create a culture in which it is OK to make mistakes but unacceptable not to identify, analyze, and learn from them."

CHAPTER 11

Event Studies

How do events, such as unexpected news, affect the price of a stock? Traders believe that having early knowledge of an impending piece of news—good or bad—provides them an information advantage that they can exploit. If they know the true value of a stock (i.e., after the effects of an event) in advance, they can buy before its price rises or sell before it falls.

But foreknowledge alone—or more likely, a strong hunch, termed *conviction* in the industry—isn't enough. Even if you are highly confident that an upcoming event will raise or lower a given stock's price, you need to forecast by how much that price will change to make a rigorous portfolio decision. And you must recognize the possibility that other investors have already accounted for the event—the news may already be "priced into" the stock. Further, how long after an event will its effects be completely "priced in," with no further effect on the stock's price? This can help an investor decide on his or her holding period following an event.

The efficient markets hypothesis (EMH) rejects the view that information can provide a durable investing advantage to varying degrees, depending on its strength (weak, semi-strong, or strong.) The EMH argues that news propagates into prices very quickly, so there are at best only very fleeting opportunities to arbitrage information discrepancies.

Event studies are a research method developed to illuminate this debate. The most comprehensive meta-study of the effects of events on stock prices was published by A.C. MacKinley in the *Journal of Economic Literature* in 1997. Its results are summarized in Figure 11.1.

MacKinley tabulated daily price data for stocks that experienced about 1,700 "events"—company-specific news items. He arrayed these data for 3 weeks (21 days) before and after the event, and computed daily price changes, averaging them among all the stocks in one of three groups:

MacKinlay: Event Studies in Economics and Finance

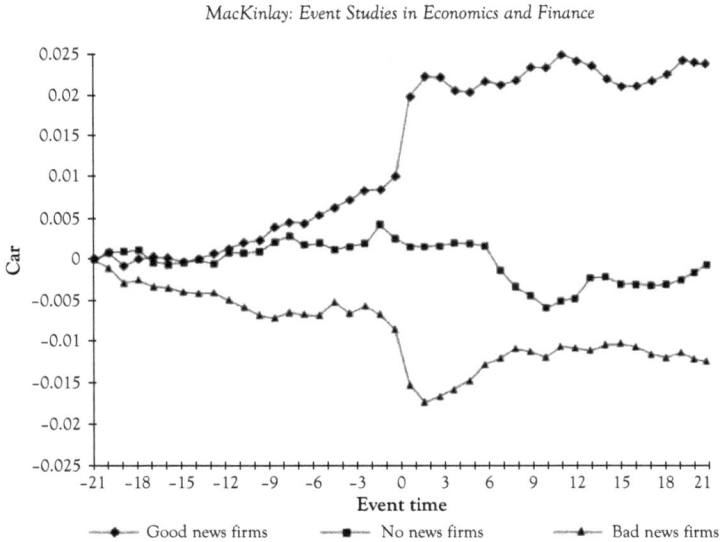

Figure 11.1 Average effects of news on stock prices
Source: MacKinlay (1997).

those that experienced good news (the top series); bad news (the bottom series); and a control group of no company-specific news (the middle series). Day 0 is the date of the event for each stock.

The first impression a viewer forms of these series is that markets react very quickly to events, and in the expected direction: Stock prices drop by an average 1.5 percent immediately after (on the day of and day after) a bad news event, and rise by 2 percent immediately after a good news event. As expected, there is no evident pattern among the control group.

But look also at the pattern in the days leading up to the event. Stock prices gradually creep upward *before* good news events, and slide downward *before* bad news events. EMH adherents argue that this corroborates their theory: Information about the impending event has leaked forward, and been traded upon, enough to consume about half the total price change that occurs from the based date until the day after the event. A counterargument is that news may simply confirm preexisting biases about a stock: Good news magnifies ongoing price gains and bad news confirms pessimism that was already driving prices lower.

Look also at the price trajectory in the weeks after events. Stocks gain further beyond the immediate event-driven price increase after good news, and recover about half the event-driven loss after bad news. These are examples of *overshoots* common in markets. As the section on arbitrage showed, investors can arbitrage overshoots, anticipating a *reversion to the mean*.

Event studies can help investors to anticipate the future trajectory of a stock's price before and after news events. While they can maximize the value of this information if they correctly anticipate an event, they can still make money after an event if they exploit knowledge about how the event will affect a stock's price.

Conducting an Event Study

Besides an optimizer, QSTK includes an event profiler. The analyst identifies the population of stocks for which he wishes to analyze the effect of events on returns. For the example in Figure 11.2 below we used all stocks in the S&P 500 (the 500 largest publicly traded U.S. companies, measured by market capitalization), for the full years of 2008 and 2009. We built an event table that indicated the dates on which company-relevant events occurred, and queried QSTK as to each stock's return relative to the market (using the SPY ETF as a proxy for the overall market) day by day before and after events. We set screens so that only stocks whose returns dropped at least 5 percent relative to the market were included in the set. This is the event we're looking to analyze. The study yielded 497 stocks and dates for which this event occurred, or about one per trading day in the 2 years. The line in Figure 11.2 shows the average relative return, with the vertical lines around it indicating their (large) standard deviation.

The results of this illustrative event study are broadly consistent with MacKinlay: About half of these stocks' cumulative excess return ebbed away in the 21 days leading up to the event, with the remainder being lost on the event day itself. Following the event, prices recovered from their event-driven overshoot, regaining about half of the event loss, with the peak excess return coming on about day 12 after the event.

This is a single illustration and should not be casually generalized—do not go out and trade based on this one example. But it illustrates the utility of event studies for developing trading strategies.

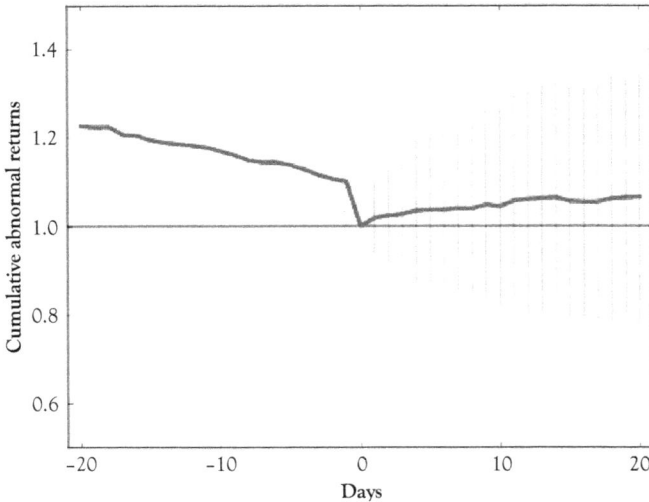

Figure 11.2 Market-relative mean return of 1704 events in 2008–2009, courtesy of Lucena Research

Assessing and Using Event Studies

Hedge funds use event studies to identify and appraise trading strategies. Commonly, analysts test out a strategy in a market simulator—a system programmed to generate price trajectories based on random combinations of historical price histories. Strategies are *backtested*—evaluated based on how they would have performed under past market conditions.

A simple example of an equity value strategy would be to buy a stock whenever its price is near the bottom of its Bollinger band—a range of plus or minus one standard deviation around its mean—while the market is near the top of its own Bollinger band. This strategy would go long in putatively underpriced stocks at a time when the overall market seemed to provide a tailwind. An event study could examine returns following events for these stocks versus returns for all other stocks.

Such studies can not only identify opportunities to generate alpha in a purely directional sense but they can also identify the optimal holding period after an event. Figure 11.2 illustrates this. The stocks affected by the 497 events studied retraced about half their losses in the 3 weeks after the event. Note how, over that time period, standard deviation rose—risk was increasing. While the maximum gain was earned at about 10 days after the event, its risk was substantially higher than at earlier points, such as 5 days after the event. It appears to the eye that the maximum risk-adjusted return (i.e., Sharpe ratio) occurred about five days after the event.

One final point about event studies that has been made before but bears repeating: Automated trading systems can be highly error prone because of faulty assumptions, or coding errors. It is always critical that a human being does a "sanity check" on study results, and on their implementation in trading strategies. When every trade is small (such that it takes thousands of trades to generate significant income), this step can be easily overlooked. But coding errors or "fat fingers" have nearly ruined several major institutions, so a human check on automatic execution can be vital.

CHAPTER 12

Overcoming Data Quirks to Design Trading Strategies

Stock price data are widely available, so you can expect that many trading strategies have already been uncovered by your competitors. Furthermore, the data you will use in performing event studies and backtesting strategies cannot be used without special care. This chapter will outline some of the main pitfalls in price data, and coping strategies to overcome those pitfalls. Our list is hardly exhaustive, but it will provide a sense of the nuances you must anticipate.

Actual Versus Adjusted Stock Price Data

Naive use of stock price data as reported by financial services—termed here *actual price data*—can be misleading. The reason is that stock prices often change for reasons that have nothing to do with market supply and demand. To properly account for the value returned by holding a stock, we must consider *splits* and *dividends issued*.

In back testing, these factors can be accounted for in a manual sort of way, provided one has a database that includes that information. However, most researchers fold the effects of these two factors into a special version of historical price called *adjusted price*. This streamlines backtesting by removing the complexity of manipulating that data.

Stock Splits

Company boards of directors occasionally believe that their stock's price has made it too expensive for some groups of investors, especially because most trades are for round lots of at least 100 shares. Options contracts are also issued to cover 100 shares at a time. A stock trading at $100 per

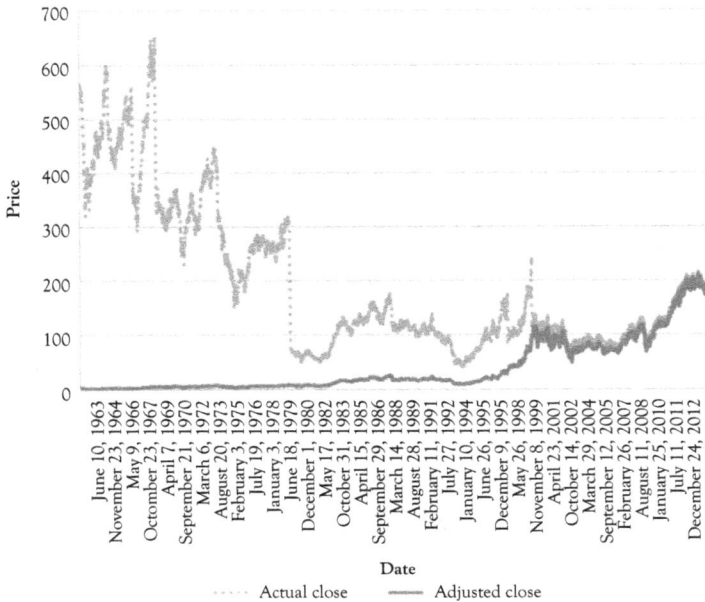

Figure 12.1 IBM's actual and split-adjusted stock price, 1963 to 2012

share would require $10,000 to open the smallest economic position—too large an amount for some retail investors. To keep the stock attractive to such purchasers, the board may elect to split the stock, dividing each old share into a larger number of new shares. The value of the company does not change, while each share is worth proportionately less (but each holder or an old share now owns N new shares [Figure 12.1]).

A 2 for 1 split, for instance, converts each old share into two new shares, so an owner of 100 shares before the split will own 200 shares after the split. But because the company's value hasn't changed, the split should not, in itself, change share values, beyond the arithmetic consequence of a split. A medium pizza is still a medium pizza, whether it is sliced into 4, 6, or 8 pieces.

Splits are infrequent, but they can still happen multiple times over a long time period. IBM, for example, has split several times in the 50 years between 1962 and 2012 (see Figure 12.1). Observe the steep drop in actual price in 1979 from about $300 per share to about $75 per share. This price change reflects a 4 for 1 split. Note that even though the price changed substantially, if you held a portion of stock before the split, the total value of that stock, and your portion of ownership of the company did not change.

Historical prices are adjusted so you can more accurately and easily evaluate how portfolio values would have grown over time.

IBM's actual 1962 share price of over $500 after adjustment corresponds to about $2.50 per share whose fractional ownership corresponds with the same fraction a share of stock confers today—an over 200-fold difference. Note that in 2012, IBM was trading for about $200, so it had appreciated about 80-fold (from $2.50 to $200) over 50 years—a 9 percent annual return.

Stock price data services adjust for splits. If on January 1, 2012, a stock split 2 for 1, then all prices prior to that date will be halved to account for the effect of the split. Where actual prices would show a 50 percent reduction in the stock price in a single day, the adjusted price would reflect the real long-term trend, independent of a split. When you conduct event studies or backtest trading strategies, it is crucial that you use prices that have been adjusted for splits.

Some boards avoid splits, probably in the belief that a high stock price will tend to attract long-term investors and discourage casual traders. As of this writing, Apple (AAPL), for example, sells for about $500 per share, making each 100-share trade worth about $50,000. Berkshire Hathaway (BRKA), Buffett's firm, has never split despite 20 percent+ annual price appreciation for nearly 50 years, and is currently priced well above $100,000 per share. However, in the mid-2000s, Berkshire created a second share class (Class "B," BRKB) priced at 1/1500th of the "A" shares.

Reverse splits are also possible. In a "reverse split"—say, 1 for 3—the stock price rises to reflect a share's increased ownership—in this example, a share controls three times as much as it did before the reverse split. A stock priced at $30 before a 1 for 3 reverse split would be priced at $90 afterward.

Dividends

Shareholders can earn income from stocks without selling them if the company board of directors declares a dividend. Dividends are a return to the shareholders of cash that is a portion of the company's annual earnings. A stock's *payout ratio* indicates this proportion. Boards can declare regular dividends (usually quarterly), or special, one-time dividends.

This means that the long-term value of owning a stock is not represented simply by its actual price, but also by the value shed over time in the terms of these dividends. The income-generating potential for a stock is measured by its dividend yield: the amount of its annual dividend per share divided by the share price. The average dividend yield presently is about 2 percent. Some companies pay dividends as high as 10 percent, and others (like BRK, or AAPL until quite recently) pay no dividend at all.

When a company pays a dividend, it distributes cash from its holdings to shareholders. So the company's assets are reduced, which typically reduces the share price by an equivalent amount. Even though the share price was reduced, the holder of the stock still captures the corresponding value. IBM share prices, note how the actual and adjusted prices differed before February 6, 2014. The difference is due to a dividend of $0.95 paid on that date.

To account for the benefit of the dividend paid on that date, we correct the adjusted price before that time proportionally. As an example, in the case of IBM's dividend of about 0.55 percent we adjust all previous, historical actual prices downward by that same amount. This ends up having the effect, in backtesting, of reaping a 0.55 percent "reward" on the date of the dividend.

Breaks in Series and Missing Data

A given stock, or all stocks, may not show price data for intervals if its trading was suspended (e.g., by its exchange), or if all trading is suspended. All trading was halted on the NASDAQ for just over 3 hours on August 22, 2013, because of faulty communications between the exchange's computers and those of the NYSE. In such situations, there will be no price data for some periods of time. Figure 12.2 shows the break in trading in the NASDAQ on that day.

Solvers such as QSTK cannot handle missing data; they will return error messages. So it is necessary to fill the data with reasonable guesses

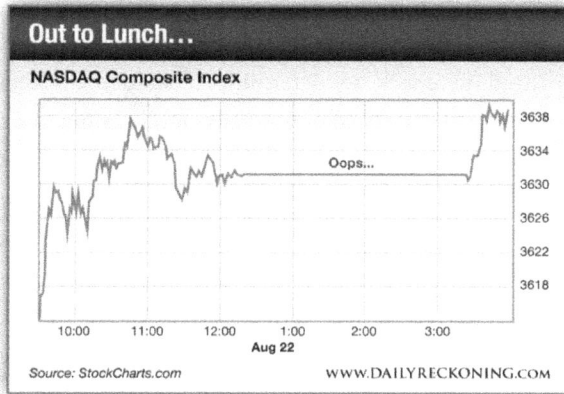

Figure 12.2 Three-hour break in NASDAQ stock price series due to unplanned trading suspension, August 22, 2013

as to what the data "would have been" if trading had occurred during the absent periods.

The common approach is to *fill forward*: to treat missing values as the same level as the last known value. So for minute-by-minute NASDAQ price data for August 22, 2013, the analyst would treat all values between 12:14 p.m. and 3:10 p.m. as the same value as at 12:13 p.m. (the last traded value). That's filling forward. as shown in Figure 12.2.

If values are missing at the beginning of the series, filling forward isn't an option. Then you would need to *fill backward*—use the first known value as also applying in the prior, missing periods.

The general rule for missing values is "fill forward first, and fill backward where you can't fill forward."

Missing Ticker Symbols

Stocks may be first listed in the middle of your time series, or delisted at some point, leading to missing data before or after the period where the stock existed. In the first instance, the company may have first gone public (begun trading its shares on an exchange). In the latter case, the company could have been acquired by another, gone private, or gone out of business entirely. Occasionally, companies change symbols; for example,

Sun Microsystems had at least three symbols in the roughly 25-year span between its listing in the 1980s and its acquisition by Oracle.

Analysts need to check to determine if sudden appearances and reappearances of symbols actually represent public company births and deaths, or merely labeling changes. For whole data sets, or for evaluations of managers, there can be a bias introduced if stocks or companies are omitted during a series. Commonly that company or fund has run into trouble, often fatal. (Hedge funds that shut down often have far underperformed their peers: according to research firm eVestment, only 30 percent of funds that existed 10 years ago are still in business today.) Analysts can scrub their sample to include only those companies that operated throughout the period, but this tends to omit more failures than successes, causing *survivor bias*.

Conclusion

These data problems are unavoidable. Capitalism is a dynamic process, which wreaks *creative destruction*—strangling poor performers, and (sometimes) buying up good performers. And market glitches happen—sometimes caused by hedge funds, as discussed in a later chapter. An analyst's goal should not be to choose a sample that avoids these data problems, because that would render his or her analysis virtually irrelevant. The challenge will be to refrain from accepting data uncritically, and also checking data for sanity.

CHAPTER 13

Data Sources

There are many sources of stock price data. The following are a few illustrative feeds with which your authors are familiar:

- Thomson Reuters Machine Readable News
- StarMine
- InsiderInsights
- Xignite
- PremiumData.net

These sources are described subsequently.

Desirable Characteristics of Datafeeds

To be really useful, a source of price or information data should have the following characteristics:

- Historical as well as current data. Without historical price data, there will be no way to evaluate or backtest strategies.
- Free of survivor bias. The data should include stocks that died or were delisted, so as to avoid survivor bias, and permit testing of predictions of demise.
- Ease of integration and use. The data source should allow for easy export to the analytical engine or database the analyst uses. QSTK, for example, can export in .csv form, for use in Excel or most database programs.
- Low latency. Once trading strategies have been tested and evaluated, they will be used, which requires near real-time data. Efficient markets arbitrage away opportunities very quickly, so delays in receiving data aren't acceptable.

Three Illustrative Information Feeds

These three are by no means the only candidates, just three with which your authors are familiar, focusing on those feeds that provide near real-time price data in addition to historic data.

- Thomson Reuters Machine Readable News: This feed delivers data with very low latency, in xml form (i.e., readily usable on other platforms). Its stories are tagged by stock symbol as positive, negative, or neutral, making it well suited to event studies.
- StarMine aggregates analysts' estimates, weighting them by past accuracy. It predicts future changes in analysts' sentiment, which the publishers claim can help predict future stock price movements. StarMine includes analysts' revisions to their reports, and publishes a feed every evening.
- InsiderInsights tabulates and reports transactions by company insiders (typically board members and senior managers). Insiders are presumed to have superior information about a company's position and prospects, so their buying or selling can be interpreted as pertinent information. Insider buying is usually construed as an unambiguous positive signal: Insiders generally buy only if they think the stock is a better investment than available alternatives. Selling by insiders need not be a negative signal, because insiders may sell simply because they have liquidity needs (college tuition, house down payment, divorce settlement, etc.) or because their portfolios are overweighted in company stock and they wish to diversify. (Financial planners argue that if your annual income derives from a company, it is foolish to allow your retirement to be equally dependent on that same company.)

Figure 13.1 shows the results of an illustrative event study conducted by Lucena Research using InsiderInsights data. There are two heavy lines;

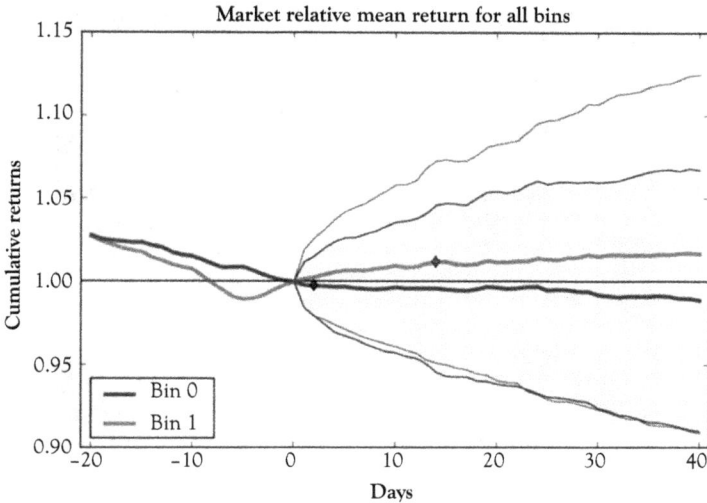

Figure 13.1 Illustrative event study
Source: Courtesy Lucena Research, LLC and InsiderInsights.com

The "Bin 0" line represents the average price of company stocks before and after an insider sale (at Day 0), with the succeeding fan showing the range of prices for different companies that experienced the event. The "Bin 1" line and fan represent insider buying. In the 21 days before the respective events, the average price fell by about 3 percent (after rebounding about 1 percent in the days immediately before the buying events). After the selling event, prices continue to modestly deteriorate, whereas they regained about 2 percent after the buying event, peaking about 15 days after the event.

These illustrate the range of data sources available, but are not meant as an endorsement.

Bio: Barton Biggs, Fairfield and Traxis Partners

Born: 1932; died 2012

Firm: Fairfield Partners, 1965 to 1973; Morgan Stanley, 1973 to 2003; Traxis Partners, Greenwich, CT, 2003 to 2012

Style: Global macro

Differentiation: SmartMoney *called Biggs "the ultimate big-picture man ... the premier prognosticator on the international scene and a mover of markets from Argentina to Hong Kong. It wouldn't be a stretch to say Biggs wrote the book on emerging-market investing." Voted the top global strategist and first in global asset allocation from 1996 to 2000 by Institutional Investor's "Investor Global Research Team" poll. Named to II's "All America Analyst Team" ten times.*

Annual return: 11.2 percent *(Fairfield Partners)*

AUM: $1.5 billion (2005)

Biggs background: He grew up in Manhattan; majored in English at Yale under Robert Penn Warren. After college he worked as a stockbroker for E.F. Hutton before founding hedge fund Fairfield Partners in 1965. He joined Morgan Stanley as an analyst in 1973, becoming its global investing strategy head in 1985. He retired from Morgan Stanley in 2003 to found Traxis.

Color: Appropriate for a creative writing graduate, Biggs was a wry and literate writer, penning four best-selling books, the last (Diary of a Hedgehog) *published posthumously in 2012. From its introduction: "The successful macro investor must be some magical mixture of an acute analyst, and investment scholar, a listener, a historian, and a riverboat gambler, and be a voracious reader. Reading is crucial."*

CHAPTER 14

Back Testing Strategies

Once a hypothesis regarding a trading strategy has been developed, prudent investors will wish to test it before committing funds to its execution. The most persuasive approach would be to *forward test*—make simulated or "paper trades" for some period of time into the future to appraise the strategy's performance versus a benchmark. But such forward testing takes time, unavoidably. An alternative is to simulate use of the tested strategy over some past period; this is back testing.

Back testing requires four main components:

- Historical data to provide the context in which the strategy will be executed in simulation.
- A definition of the strategy that can be automated.
- A market simulator that represents the simulated trades. Ideally, it should include transactions costs such as commissions, as well as *market impact* costs (the effect on a stock's market price of increased trading volume caused by our strategy).
- An analysis engine that records the returns from the simulated trades and compares the strategy's performance versus a benchmark.

With these pieces, an analyst can step history forward a day at a time, see if conditions trigger buying or selling under the strategy being tested, and evaluate the strategy's return and variability (risk). Figure 14.1 below illustrates an analysis report by Lucena Research for an example strategy, in light gray line shows when the strategy sold or bought, and how its return and its risk compared to buying and holding the S&P 500 in dark line (usually considered the default reference strategy.) In terms of cumulative return, this particular strategy outperformed the benchmark substantially for the evaluation period. You can see by the history graph

Performance Metrics			
Change In Fund Value Since Inception:			
Portfolio	Initial	Final	Return
Fund	$100,000K	$174,880K	$74,880K
Benchmark	$100,000K	$136,597K	$36,597K

Performance metrics since inception:			
Portfolio	Return	Sharpe	Sortino	Alpha
Fund	74.88%	0.50	0.62	0.51
Benchmark	36.60%	0.27	0.34	0.00

Transaction costs since inception:	
Number of transactions	7,766
Commissions	$0.00
Slippage	$0.00
Borrowing Costs	$0.00
Total Transaction Costs	$0.00

Risk since inception:		
Portfolio	StdDev.	Max D-Down
Fund	0.95%	-41.73%
Benchmark	1.35%	-56.78%

Benchmark: S&P 500

Figure 14.1 Sample results of a back test. The strategy performance is shown in light gray, with benchmark in dark

Source: Lucena Research.

that it was also much less volatile. These factors combine to provide a significantly improved Sharpe ratio of 0.50 versus 0.27 for the benchmark. It is also common for hedge funds to provide lower cumulative returns compared to a benchmark, but also with significantly reduced volatility. This relative performance is common to the claims of many hedge funds: their strategies have lower volatility and lower returns in rising markets, presumably because of the performance drag caused by hedges. But their risk-adjusted return-as measured by their Sharpe ratio or information ratio-is superior to unhedged long-only strategies.

Cautions About Back Testing

Any statistical method can be seductive—it is easy to overinterpret positive results when a strategy is evaluated. Arguably, several of the major hedge fund blowups have occurred because back testing was accepted without skepticism. Here is a short list of common pitfalls.

- *"Peeking" into the future*: You know the actual history of financial markets, which a contemporary from your back testing period would not. You can choose a strategy that is, at least unconsciously, designed for those conditions. It is important to make sure that the period from which you drew your inspiration in designing the tested strategy is not the same as the period from which your back testing data come. Otherwise, you are simply confirming a tautology.

- *Data mining*: The "data mining fallacy" arises when an analyst tests many strategies and, inevitably, finds one that is very successful in the testing period—but falls flat on its face in another testing period. The strategy was inadvertently optimized for unique circumstances or random noise. If you cannot identify any plausible theory to explain why a given strategy worked so well under a test, there is a good chance its success is a data mining anomaly—you "mined the data" until you found a spurious relationship.

- *A changing market*: Market conditions change—in fact, that is a central premise of the efficient market hypothesis: market actors continually adapt to other actors' strategies, which drives this change. A strategy tested in a past period may reflect very different conditions from those you face today. If you back tested strategies with historical data from the late 1990s, for example, a leveraged long-only strategy heavily overweighted in Internet stocks would look like a huge winner. Unfortunately, after the dot com bubble came the bust, and tech stocks have not performed nearly so well since.

A common protection from these common problems is to cross validate the tested strategy. Cross validation means testing the strategy on more than one subset of historical data to see if results are similar in each subset. You could test the strategy with two subsets of stocks, or two subsets of time periods. If you get strong results in only one of the subsets, it is likely that those results are not valid—they have happened because of one of these pitfalls.

Bio: Michael Steinhardt, Steinhardt Partners

Born: 1940

Firm: Steinhardt Partners

Founded: 1967, as Steinhardt, Fine, Berkowitz, & Co (1967 to 1979); Steinhardt Partners (1979 to 1995).

Style: Equity long/short, frequently heavily hedged (i.e., net short).

Differentiation: Early users of monetary data to predict stock market movements; "block trading" in opaque "third markets" (i.e., outside of exchanges) that provided institutions needed liquidity in exchange for small discounts to market prices.

Steinhardt background: Son of Sol Steinhardt, a stolen jewelry "fence," high-stakes gambler, and confederate of prominent Mafiosi (he dined with Albert Anastasia the night before he was gunned down). After attending Wharton, Steinhardt became a junior analyst at mutual fund Calvin Bullock, then at Loeb, Rhoades & Co. His initial stake came from envelopes of cash invested from his father's gambling winnings. Founded the partnership in 1967 with early investments from William Salomon, founder of Salomon Brothers; and Jack Nash, founder of Odyssey Partners.

Annual return: 24.5 percent after fees. Fees were at or below industry norms: 1 percent of AUM, with performance fees at 15 percent of gains (realized or unrealized), later raised to 20 percent.

AUM (peak): $4.5 billion (1994)

Color: "He was short, barrel-chested, and prone to terrifying outbursts....He would let forth a blood-curdling torrent of abuse and then his temples would turn red....If there was one quality that Steinhardt valued in people, it was the balls to take a position" (from More Money Than God*).*

PART IV
Case Study and Issues

CHAPTER 15

Hedge Fund Case Study: Long Term Capital Management (LTCM)

The yin and the yang of hedge fund experience is revealed in the short, dramatic life of Long Term Capital Management. In its five brief years, it reached the apex of hedge fund success—spectacular returns, clamorous investors, and extremes of arrogance and conspicuous consumption. When the end came suddenly, the corpse was preserved on life support temporarily, to harvest its organs. But Long Term Capital Management's (LTCM) true believers—its partners and employees, who had invested their life savings in the fund—were mostly wiped out.

This story illustrates the life cycle of a very successful, then spectacularly doomed, hedge fund. It is drawn from several sources, particularly Lowenstein's '*When Genius Failed* and Lewis's "How the Eggheads Cracked."

Origins: JM (John Meriwether)

John Meriwether ran the "quant arbitrage" desk at Salomon Brothers in the late 1980s and early 1990s, and was instrumental in the securitization movement in the prior decade (described colorfully in Lewis's *Liar's Poker*). He had a reputation as a superb developer of talent, and an early adopter of "quant" strategies—trading strategies that use extensive data analysis to identify systematic relationships between the prices of assets, in order to exploit deviations that occur. At the quant desk, he built a staff of "rocket scientists"—mathematicians and scientists who had little financial experience but world-class statistical abilities; they fit poorly in the fraternity or club world of Wall Street. Their unit generated most of Salomon's profits each year in the late 1980s and early 1990s, and Meriwether secured them a guarantee of 15 percent of all profits generated. When he was tarnished in an internal scandal in the early 1990s, Meriwether formed his own hedge fund, LTCM, capitalizing it at the then-unheard-of sum of $2.5 billion.

The LTCM team possessed an exceptional pedigree. Two of its senior members were finance academic superstars: Robert Merton of Harvard and Myron Scholes of the University of Chicago. Along with Fisher Black, Scholes authored the Black–Scholes formula, the definitive method of pricing options. Merton and Scholes each shared in Nobel prizes in economics. The LTCM team also included former Federal Reserve vice chair David Mullins; early investors included many of the leaders of white shoe Wall Street firms.

The Rise

With a stellar reputation came exceptional pricing power. LTCM demanded, and got, deep trading discounts from clearing brokers, and the lowest interest rates on borrowed money—the latter especially valuable when the fund borrowed as much as $30 for every dollar in equity. Such high rates of leverage were unheard of in the hedge fund world, although not uncommon in commercial banking. LTCM's partners were comfortable with leverage because they were convinced that their investments had as little risk as those of regulated commercial banks.

At first, in 1994, this seems to have been true. The team's core skills pertained to fixed income arbitrage: betting on systematic differences in the pricing of bonds. For example, they would execute a "paired trade" in which they would short (bet against) newly issued Treasuries of a particular maturity, while going long in seasoned (less recently issued) securities of the same maturity. The trade was premised on the expectation that the prices of the newer versions of the security, which were more liquid, would be bid up; while the older versions were depressed. Eventually, this anomaly would resolve and price relationships would be restored. Such disparities might be very small, so profits mandated that high volumes be traded, using borrowed money (i.e., high leverage). LTCM earned returns approaching 100 percent per year in 1994 and 1995, and seemed to do no wrong. Partners oozed arrogance and demanded ever tougher terms from the firm's suppliers and counterparties.

Success bred overconfidence. By 1996, the firm began to dabble in convertible arbitrage (buying convertible bonds and shorting the issuer's stock, in the belief that the two assets prices would converge), and then straight equity arbitrage. By late 1996, the firm's portfolio included increasing volumes of derivatives: equity options and interest rate swaps. For every dollar in equity, the firm had positions of $200 or more in derivatives.

By 1997 the partners were tired of sharing their seemingly limitless gains with clients, and they began returning client investments. By late in the year, nearly all of the remaining equity was owned by LTCM's partners or employees. While this had the unintended consequence of protecting some former investors from the blowup of the summer of 1998, it also shrank the fund's equity base and left it less able to absorb those blows.

The Fall

Even in 1998, a large portion of LTCM's portfolio was based on fixed-income arbitrage positions—expectations that anomalous spreads among different bonds would right themselves, given time. But when Russia unexpectedly defaulted in the summer of 1998, things began to unravel. As investors rushed to the safety of Treasuries, "irrational" spreads became magnified. The partners at LTCM felt, that given time, things would rectify as they always had before, but time was an asset that LTCM lacked. LTCM also lacked the capital to buy more time for them to rectify. Lenders issued margin calls, demanding that LTCM liquefy positions, regardless of losses, to deliver cash. As Keynes once said, "The market can remain irrational longer than you can remain solvent."

As LTCM's portfolio collapsed and lenders demanded their cash back, clearing brokers prepared to cease processing LTCM's trades. This would have rendered the fund completely illiquid, and under the circumstances, insolvent. Because so many top institutions had investments in the fund, which they had in turn pledged as collateral for their own loans, it was believed that if LTCM failed, it could take down many other financial institutions as well. The New York Federal Reserve Bank convened a consortium of Wall Street banks to put LTCM into receivership: they loaned it about $300 million in bridge financing for the express purpose of unwinding the firm's portfolio and shutting it down. Three of the government officials involved in creating that consortium were shown on the cover of *Time* magazine, dubbed, "The Committee to Save the World."

The process took about 18 months, so LTCM staggered on into 2000. A final tally of its losses included those from an eclectic array of strategies:

Traditional fixed-income arbitrage losses:

- Yield curve arbitrage: $215 million
- Developed country directional trades (i.e., unhedged): $371 million
- Emerging markets, including Russia: $430 million
- High-yield bond arbitrage: $100 million

Equity and related arbitrage losses:

- Equity pairs: $286 million
- S&P 500 stocks: $203 million
- Merger arbitrage: roughly even

Derivatives losses:

- Interest rate swaps: $1.6 billion
- Equity volatility (options, futures): $1.3 billion

LTCM had nearly $4 billion in equity at the beginning of 1998. It could have absorbed the losses associated with its traditional arbitrage strategies, and probably even its extensions into equity arbitrage. The killing blows came from derivatives.

The Aftermath

LTCM ceased to be by early 2000. Meriwether established a new boutique hedge fund within months: JMW partners. Most of the partners rebuilt their lives in other investment operations, although they lost the vast majority of their net worth when LTCM imploded. As noted earlier, ironically, LTCM's partners' arrogance inadvertently protected most of their investors, who had money forcibly returned to them in 1997.

This same pattern was repeated on an even larger scale in 2008 in a number of Wall Street institutions. Ironically, the experience that many of those leaders had in the LTCM debacle of 1998 helped prepare them for a crisis two orders of magnitude larger a decade later.

Bio: George Soros, Quantum Fund

Born: 1930, Budapest, Hungary

Firm: Quantum Fund (since 1978); Soros Fund (1973 to 1978); Double Eagle Fund (1969 to 1973)

Cofounders: Jim Rogers; Stanley Druckenmiller (each later left Soros and formed their own funds)

Style: Pioneer of global macro

Annual return: Over 20 percent (1969 to 2010)

AUM: $27.9 billion (2011)

Differentiation: Soros is extraordinarily well connected in both financial and government circles, giving him an insight—and possibly inside information—into likely actions of major corporations and governments. Known as "the man who broke the Bank of England," he bet in 1992 that Britain could no longer maintain the pound's value against the Deutschmark; his shorts of the pound earned $1.8 billion in profits in one week in September.

Soros background: Born of a well-to-do Jewish family in Budapest; Emigrated to the UK in 1949 to study at the London School of Economics. Spurned by City firms, his first financial job was an entry-level position at a brokerage firm run by Hungarian émigrés. Moving to New York in 1956, Soros migrated into research, rising to be the head of research for Wall Street brokerage Arnhold and S. Bleichroder in 1967. Left to found Double Eagle fund—the double eagle was the symbol of the Austro-Hungarian empire—in 1969.

Color: Soros is a protégé of philosopher Karl Popper, naming one of his charities the Open Society Institute in honor of Popper's masterwork, The Open Society and Its Enemies. A prolific author, he promotes his theory of "reflexivity"—the idea that little can be predicted with assurance because humans will react to conditions to make predictions self-cancelling. Soros is a prominent philanthropist, including to the Democratic Party and its candidates.

CHAPTER 16

Opportunities and Challenges for Hedge Funds

Hedge funds transitioned from a niche industry in the 1980s catering to small number of wealthy families, to an almost mainstream asset class in the portfolios of most large institutional investors (pension funds, endowments, etc). By the 2000s, these funds reached a magnitude nearly commensurate with traditional assets, equities, and bonds—managing about two and a half trillion dollars by 2014. Today there are nearly as many hedge funds as there are mutual funds.

But hedge funds' move from the margins to the center of the investing world pose new challenges for the industry. This chapter briefly outlines several of the main challenges and opportunities hedge funds will face in the coming years.

Performance

Any investment product's *raison d'etre* is performance, or at least risk-adjusted performance. In their original incarnation under A. W. Jones, hedge funds *hedged,* compensating for issue-specific risk by hedging away systematic (market) risk. For example, a fund might go long a particular stock, and sell short the market index that drives that stock's beta. Many funds aspire to be "market neutral," or to achieve *absolute* return—positive returns above the rate of inflation regardless of the market's direction.

As a group, hedge funds have failed to meet this standard. The HFRI index that tracks aggregate hedge fund performance lagged the S&P 500 for eight of the ten years prior to the 2008 market crash. A low-cost stock index fund would have produced superior results. While hedge funds did not fall quite as far as indexes in 2008, they still were soundly drubbed. For the five years from the summer of 2008 through 2013, the composite

HFRI index produced 3.4 percent annualized returns, versus 7.3 percent for the S&P 500 and 4.9 percent for the Barclay's U.S. Aggregate Bond Index. This five-year period includes the 40 percent+ swoon in late 2008 and the subsequent sharp recovery in 2009 and thereafter. For the 15 years from 2000 to 2014, the HFRI Composite trailed a standard 60/40 indexed portfolio such as Vanguard's Balanced Index Fund by 28 percent (72 percent cumulative return for HFRI versus 100 percent for the balanced fund).

Poor average performance need not be the death knell of an investing style—if it did, few actively managed stock mutual funds would still be in business. But it will probably lead to shorter holding periods for investors (as they change funds in search of performance). More skeptical investors will lead to shorter fund life spans. It can bring significant bifurcation in pricing: downward pressure on prices for the substandard performers and great pricing power for the rare strong performers.

Pricing

"Two and twenty"—the classic hedge fund fee structure is already an endangered species. Many hedge funds are already segmenting their customer base; offering superior terms—lower prices or a shorter lockup period—to early or large investors. As an example, in July 2013, Merchants' Gate Capital lowered its AUM fee from the 1.5 to 2 percent it had charged since its founding in 2007 to 1.25 to 1.75 percent. It manages $2 billion in its equity fund. Kopernick Capital's long–short fund launched in 2013 charges a 0.25 percent AUM fee. Even firms with superior pricing power aren't immune: Caxton Associates' AUM fee has been cut from 3 percent to 2.6 percent.

Incentive fees have likewise been under pressure. The aforementioned Caxton lowered its fee to 27.5 percent of profits from a previous 30 percent. Industry-wide, average incentive fees have slowly fallen from the low 19 percent range of annual profits to 18.4 percent in the first quarter of 2013, according to HFR. A Goldman Sachs survey for 2012 reports nearly identical findings: 1.65 percent AUM fee and 18.3 percent performance fee.

Fund company profitability may not be declining proportionate to performance fee rates, because financial repression—artificially low interest rates engineered by central banks—has also lowered the "hurdle rate" above which excess investing profits are calculated and fees exacted.

Nevertheless, the frequency with which hedge fund management generates new billionaires among those managers probably peaked before the 2008 crash. Achieving high absolute profits will probably require the gathering of more assets, since both excess performance and high performance fees will be increasingly rare. Clients are already demanding less pay for poor performance. This may lead to a long-overdue industry shakeout and consolidation.

Regulation: Fund Registration and Marketing

U.S. regulators generally have a bias against hedge funds, and have only allowed them so much freedom because of protection provided by their allies in Congress. Some restrictions have lately been lifting. For example, the 2013 Jumpstart Our Business Startups (JOBS) Act liberalized the terms under which new firms may seek investment capital, allowing some start-ups to bypass financial intermediaries entirely. (The most common manifestation is Kickstarter campaigns.) SEC regulations promulgated in the summer of 2013 pursuant to the JOBS Act will permit hedge funds to advertise. A registration requirement has been nominally extant for several years, but never really enforced by the SEC.

However, in time, hedge funds may face an increasingly onerous regulatory environment. Mutual funds are governed by the "40 Act" (Investment Company Act of 1940) and similar laws may be brewing for hedge funds. This will probably be a salutary development: It will force standardization of reporting that has been advocated by authorities such as the CFA Institute, but cannot be mandated. The expense of meeting these regulations may prove to be too much for smaller hedge funds. On the other hand, greater transparency should accelerate some of the client-friendly developments mentioned elsewhere in this chapter.

Finally, this new regulatory climate may eventually lead to broader investor access to hedge funds. Currently they are prohibited from accepting monies from other than accredited investors. But this is a largely meaningless restriction, since there are many retail products offered by financial services institutions that already invest in hedge funds, including employer-sponsored retirement plans. Millions of nonaccredited investors already have exposure to this asset class, at least indirectly. Pimco, for instance, which runs the world's largest bond mutual fund (Pimco Total Return Fund, assets $262 billion), recently announced a new fund that will employ hedge fund strategies, but have a minimum investment of only $1,000 and $50 for additional investments. *Morningstar* reports that the assets in "alternative" mutual funds more than tripled between 2008 and August 2013: from $35 billion to $118 billion. Thirty-six alternative mutual funds were launched in the first eight months of August 2013, more than during the same period during any of the previous 10 years.

Regulation: Insider Trading

Stung by charges of laxity during the buildup to the 2007 to 2008 financial crisis, the government has become far more aggressive in prosecuting securities violations. The crime most pertinent to hedge funds is insider trading. Hedge funds that practice event-driven or macroinvesting strategies have a particular need for insight into how key corporate and governmental actors think and will act. Sometimes fund personnel have engaged in schemes, many quite elaborate, to compensate insiders for investment-relevant information. As this book is being written two senior officials at SAC Capital have been convicted of insider trading, and the firm itself is under indictment. Founder Steve Cohen has not been charged. But even the taint of suspicion can deal a mortal blow to a financial institution, because it can scare away lenders and counterparties. This has been the story behind the precipitate fall of many institutions, including LTCM in 1998 and Lehmann in 2008. SAC has announced it will return all outside investors' capital and reestablish itself as a family office.

Hedge funds whose "edge" depends on superior privileged information flow will find their competitive advantage deeply eroded by more rigorous enforcement of the law. Even for those not directly affected, they may find their access to capital severely impaired.

Regulation: Systemic Importance

The 2007 to 2008 financial crisis did not originate in hedge funds: Mallaby argues that in fact the funds exercised a moderating influence. Arguably, it was a banking crisis, with the epicenter being those who originated subprime mortgages or who leveraged holdings of mortgage-backed securities (MBS). The extent of these banks' interconnections with other financial counterparties was such that several were deemed "systemically important"—their failure would bring down other, sounder institutions. Being "too big to fail" engendered a multi-hundred-billion-dollar rescue, the Troubled Asset Relief Program (TARP). But ongoing attempts at regulatory reform may also address the "shadow banking system"—institutions that lend, yet are not banks—like hedge funds.

The 2010 Dodd-Frank financial reform law made only marginal changes to the legal environment for hedge funds. But there is a growing backlash in policy circles that it and other reform measures preserved too much of the status quo. Arguably, one of the first casualties of this backlash was Larry Summers's expected nomination to be the next chairman of the Federal Reserve System, to succeed Ben Bernanke. Summers withdrew his candidacy in mid-September 2013 in the face of evident opposition from Democrats who planned to use his hearings to air multiple grievances about the financial deregulation he supported in the late 1990s, and the extremely limited reforms he helped enact in the late 2000s.

Hedge funds have friends in high places, so it would be foolish to assume that they will be seriously harmed by a rising tide of reregulation. But it seems like that at the margin the climate will become more constraining, especially regarding leverage levels or use of derivatives in trading strategies—both seen as key culprits in 2007 to 2008.

Front-Running

As noted in earlier chapters, some of institutions' competitive advantage comes from early access to market order data (the order book), by collocating servers at exchanges and having dedicated high-speed communications that shave milliseconds off order processing. This allows these institutions, including hedge funds, to "see into the future" (albeit by only microseconds) to exploit that information to front-run the market. Such an advantage is tiny and fleeting; however, if the hedge funds trade fast enough and often enough (turbocharged by leverage), profits can accumulate into significant sums. Experts estimate that 70 to 80 percent of the daily trading volume on major exchanges is high-frequency trading (HFT).

While it is argued that HFT increases the market's efficiency, it has two deleterious side effects: First, it sometimes aggravates volatility. At least two recent major incidents have been traced to HFT: the October 1987 crash, caused by "program trading" (the then-current term for what is now called HFT), and the May 2010 "flash crash." (Several other lesser known hiccups, such as the NASDAQ's three-hour suspension of trading in July 2013, were caused by software or user problems, not HFT.) Volatility can provide a profit opportunity for financial engineers (such as derivatives salesmen) and traders, but it scares off individual investors.

Second, HFT delegitimizes financial markets. This is a key tenet of Michael Lewis's recent book on HFT, *Flash Boys*. A pillar of legitimacy is investor belief in a level playing field: that relevant information is readily available to anyone smart enough to seek and use it. This is why exchange listing privileges have financial reporting requirements: so that all investors can see a company's true financial condition before investing. But an individual investor trading in an HFT world is like a poker player who knows that some other players can see his cards: there is an information asymmetry to the disadvantage of the individual.

For example, a common technique for limiting losses is a stop loss rule. An investor may specify that an investment should be sold automatically if its price falls below some relative value threshold. For example, he or she might sell when the asset's price falls 25 percent below his or her entry price, or 25 percent below the last peak price (the latter is called a "25 percent trailing stop"). The width of the stop can be expanded or contracted to account for the asset's expected volatility and the investor's risk tolerance. Such rules can be very effective for limiting losses. But because of the prevalence of HFT, investment advisers *counsel against entering stop losses into the market* (i.e., placing a contingent sell limit order with your broker). Advisers argue that HFT traders who see the order book can place sell orders to drive an asset's price below your stop threshold, triggering your stop (and those of other investors). They can then buy the asset at this depressed price. The HFT trader has taken advantage of an information asymmetry: knowing your trading rule.

But serious regulation of HFT seems unlikely. Trading volume can migrate across borders quite easily, and will flow to the most lightly regulated exchange. And such a technical process as HFT cannot avoid "regulatory lag"—the fact that regulators, who are reactive, will always be behind financial innovators, who act opportunistically.

Private Exchanges and Dark Pools

Dark pools are individual firms or groups of firms that trade shares among themselves to avoid exchange fees and to accelerate trading. They are largely unregulated, and therefore less transparent than major exchanges.

These pools are extensions of the internal markets that brokerage firms have long maintained. If Client A wishes to sell a stock and Client B wishes to buy the same stock, the broker performs a service by matching them up internally, without using a stock exchange. Dark pools widen the trading universe to the clients of all the firms in the pool, but far less than all the firms that trade on the exchange.

Any regulatory attempt to force all trading onto regulated exchanges will be nullified by technology and the inventiveness of intermediaries. Instead, it is likely that in time SEC and other regulators' reach will extend into dark pools. But it is also certain that brokers and investors will innovate new forms to stay ahead of the reach of regulators.

Conclusion

There are persistent incentives to innovate in finance: in products, in business forms, and in regulatory avoidance. Hedge funds experienced a heyday in the 1990s and early 2000s, as new investing styles (e.g., quant arbitrage) made superior profits, and new technologies (e.g., collocated servers and fiber optic communications) allowed more front running. But financial markets are also highly efficient, and these profits are being competed away—in part because the 2008 meltdown called into question the cost-effectiveness of many hedge funds. Pricing trends follow those of other asset classes such as brokerage commissions or mutual fund expense ratios.

While there will always be successful new funds boasting of exciting new strategies (like LTCM in the mid-1990s), the average fund will be a less profitable place than it was for the past few decades. Hedge funds may increasingly resemble mutual funds, which as noted earlier, may present more good than bad to individual investors.

Teaching Cases

All cases are available from Harvard Business School Press, www.hbsp.com

Part I, Chapter 2; and Part IV: Chapters 14 and 15

Matrix Capital Management
Highbridge Capital Management: Building a Sustainable Organization
Man Group (A)

Part I, Chapter 3

Fixed Income Arbitrage in a Financial Crisis (A): U.S. Treasuries in November 2008

Part I, Chapter 5; and Part II: Chapters 6, 7, 8

Boston Properties (A)
Cypress Semiconductor Corporation and SunPower Corporation
Citigroup's Exchange Offer
Nikkei 225 Reconstitution
Convertible Bonds of Countrywide Financial Corporation
Extraordinary Value Partners, LLC

Part III: Chapter 9

Martingale Asset Management LP in 2008, 130/30 Funds, and a Low-Volatility Strategy

Glossary

We thank the students in Tucker Balch's online course Computational Investing, Part 1, for their assistance in compiling this glossary.

Alpha: A measure of an investment style's incremental return relative to simply holding a diversified portfolio. All active management, such as hedge funds, strives for "positive alpha."

Arbitrage: Buying a near-identical asset in one market and selling it in a different market at a higher price. This opportunity to profit will usually be exploited by profit-seeking investors, who, through their buying and selling, will "arbitrage away" price disparities.

(Arithmetical) Average rate of return: An asset's **return on investment** averaged over multiple periods. If the S&P 500 returned 10 percent 3 years ago, 7 percent 2 years ago, and 1 percent last year, the average annual rate of return over the three years is $(10 + 7 + 1 = 18) \div 3 = 6$ percent per year. Strictly speaking, this is an arithmetic average: summing the returns and dividing the sum by the number of years. A superior approach that accounts for the effects of compounding is a geometric average, the **compound annual growth rate (CAGR)**.

Asset allocation: Specifying the desired fraction of a portfolio to be invested in a given class of assets. For example, a "balanced" allocation might be 50 percent equities and 50 percent bonds. Allocations can change gradually, as the investor's time horizon shortens; or quickly, to respond to changes in relative valuations.

AUM: Assets under management. Wealth managers, including hedge funds, charge fees based on the amount of clients' assets they manage.

Bear market: A sustained period in which the general direction of the price of a class of assets is downward. For contrast, see **correction**, **rally**, and **bull market**.

Beta: A measure of a financial instrument's (like a stock) **volatility** relative to the broader universe of similar instruments. For example, a stock's beta is the ratio of its standard deviation to the standard deviation of a broad stock index such as the S&P 500. A beta of less than 1.0 is associated with a low volatility stock such as an electric utility. A beta of above 1.0 might mean a small-cap or growth stock, where investors overreact to both good and bad news. A beta of 1.0 implies a stock with volatility equal to the index.

Bollinger Bands: Range around an asset's price on a given day that reflects one standard deviation above and below that price.

Bonds: An investment that pays the buyer a stream of coupon payments at a specified interest rate. Also known as a "fixed income" investment. The price of bonds moves inversely with their interest rate.

Bull market: A sustained period of upward movement in the price of an asset class. Bull markets can be punctuated by **corrections**.

Capital Assets Pricing Model (CAPM): Framework that distinguishes investment returns of an asset between market returns (beta) and asset-specific returns (alpha).

Capital gain: The part of an asset's **total return** that occurs because of changes in its price, as opposed to from **dividend** payments. Capital gains are sometimes taxed at favorable (lower) rates than is ordinary income such as wage income.

Compound annual growth rate (CAGR): Annual growth based on the geometric average, not the arithmetic average. Using the example from "average growth rate," the CAGR would be [(1.10) × (1.07) × (1.01) = 1.1877] raised to the one-third power (to reflect 3 years of compounding = 1.05933, or a 5.933 percent CAGR. In this example, the result is very close to the arithmetic mean of 6 percent, but with larger growth rates or more years, the arithmetic and geometric means can diverge significantly. CAGRs are the superior way to compute and asset's long-term **return on investment (ROI)**. For a simple way to roughly compute CAGRs in your head, *see* also the **Rule of 72.**

Compounding: The exponential effect of persistent growth. One hundred dollars deposited into mutual fund that grows at a 5 percent rate of compounding will be worth $105 at the end of the first year, $110.25 after the second year, $121.62 after the fifth year, and $155.13 after the 10th year. Higher rates will compound even faster. Compounding can make the job of saving a given amount much easier if the saver starts early enough, because its effects are magnified over time.

Constraint: Limitation on flexibility that restricts the optimum solution. *See* also **optimization.**

Correction: An interruption in a bull market or rally in which an asset's class's prices fall (by convention, by at least 10 percent). **Bull** and **bear markets** need not reflect a uniform rise or fall in asset prices; they can be interrupted by corrections (downward) or **rallies** (upward).

Correlation: A measure of the relationship between two variables. In the context of investing, correlations are used to represent the degree to which asset class A (say, stocks) moves in tandem with asset class B (say, bonds). If A rises whenever B rises, the two assets have a high **positive correlation**. Investors seek to hold assets that move in opposite directions, that is, that have a high **negative correlation**, so that when A falls, B rises and compensates for (hedges against) the effects of the drop in A. This smoothes out fluctuations in the combined portfolio value of A and B together. Correlations are measured on a scale from -1.0 (perfect negative correlation—A always rises when B falls, and vice versa) to 1.0 (perfect positive correlation). *See* also **decoupling**.

Cumulative rate of return: The accumulated returns achieved by an asset over a specified period. If $1,000 in 2005 grows to $2,000 by 2010, it achieved a 100 percent cumulative growth rate for those 5 years. Its **compound** *annual* **growth rate (CAGR)** would be 14.9 percent per year.

Deviation, standard: *See* Standard deviation and variance. A measure of an asset price's volatility.

Diversification: Avoiding putting all your "eggs" in only one "basket." Diversification of an individual's investment portfolio means holding several classes of assets (not only stocks or only bonds), as well as multiple securities in the class (e.g., owning stock shares in several different companies). Commercial transactions may diversify the currency used (e.g., including euros or yen as well as dollars). Diversification smoothes out fluctuations in value—as long as the assets that are added fluctuate based on different causes than the original ones. See also **correlation**. For a contrasting view, see **fundamental law.**

Dividend: A portion of a corporation's earnings paid to its stockholders. A company's "dividend payout rate" is that proportion. Stocks can be compared by their dividend yields (dollars of dividend per share divided by the purchase price of the share). Many academic studies have found that the vast majority of stocks' **total return** comes from dividends.

Efficient frontier: In a scatter graph showing the risk and returns of various asset classes, the efficient frontier displays the subset for which there are no superior assets—where higher return requires taking higher risk. It is a generally curved frontier above and to the left of the majority of assets.

Equities: Common **stocks**, so called because their owner holds a share of the company's "stockholder's equity" (net worth).

ETFs: Exchange-traded funds; mutual fund–like investment pools that invest in a particular class of security, such as stocks of companies located in a particular country or a specific industrial sector. When they originated, ETFs were passively managed funds with commensurately low costs. As their numbers have proliferated, ETFs are becoming less diversified and more expensive.

Fundamental Law: In the 1980s, Richard Grinold introduced what he calls the Fundamental Law of Active Investing, described nicely in his book cowritten with Ronald Kahn. (See "Suggestions for Further Reading." We paraphrase his law as follows:

$$\text{performance} = \text{skill} * \sqrt{\text{breadth}}$$

Skill is a measure of how well a manager transforms information about an equity into an accurate prediction of future return, and *breadth* represents the number of investment decisions (trades) the manager makes each year.

Gross domestic product (GDP): The total goods and services produced in an economy. The U.S. GDP, at nearly $15 trillion, is about 25 percent of world GDP. **GDP per capita** is a measure of the standard of living: a nation's GDP divided by the size of its population. The U.S. GDP per capita is among the highest in the world. Gross national product (GNP) is GDP plus the net effect of the balance of payments (surplus or deficit).

Gross margin: One definition of margin also known as "profit." Gross margin is revenues minus only those costs directly related to the production of the company's product, such as raw materials. Net margin, or the "bottom line," also deducts company-wide costs such as overhead. Margins are often expressed as a percentage of company revenues to make them comparable across companies.

Inflation: An increase in the general level of prices, usually measured by the consumer price index. Put another way, an indication that the supply of money is growing faster than demand for it (i.e., than overall economic activity). This oversupply of money causes it to decline in value. This is reflected in higher prices for the things money buys, that is, inflation. As Nobel Prize–winning economist Milton Friedman noted, "inflation is always and everywhere a *monetary* phenomenon" (emphasis added).

Leverage: The use of other people's money to purchase an asset. An example is a homeowner who secures a mortgage from a bank to buy a house. Because the bank has loaned funds (as opposed to purchased an equity share of the house), the borrower experiences the full effect of price movements in the asset. When the asset's price is rising, the borrower enjoys the full gain; but the same is true if the asset price falls. The recent recession was largely caused because major banks had used massive leverage—sometimes borrowing more than $30 for every dollar of equity they had—to purchase assets such as mortgage-backed securities (MBSs). When the MBSs fell in price because of rising defaults, the banks suffered magnified losses because of the extent of their leverage. The late 2000s recession was long because households were obliged to **deleverage** (a.k.a. "unwind") their heavily indebted positions.

Long/short: A hedging strategy that takes a long position in one asset and a short position in another. For example, a fund might be convinced that, say, Exxon had good prospects, and buy XOM; and at the same time, it would hedge against a general decline in the oil industry by going short an oil ETF. A.W. Jones' original "hedged fund" pioneered long/short strategies. Many hedge funds fall between the poles of "long only" and "short only" with such mixed strategies.

Marginal tax rate: The tax rate collected on your next dollar of income (i.e., "at the margin"). High marginal rates are believed to discourage the earning of additional income, because the earner keeps little of their new earnings.

Market cap: Short for "market capitalization" or the current value stock markets place on an entire company. If a company has one million shares outstanding that traded today at $6 per share, it has a market cap of $6 million. Companies are categorized as "large cap," "midcap," and "small cap." There is no standard definition of the breakpoints between the categories, but a rough rule of thumb is above $10 billion, $1 billion to 10 billion, and below $1 billion, respectively. "Microcaps," as the name implies, are even smaller than small caps with a market cap in the millions, not billions.

Modern portfolio theory (MPT): Principles of portfolio design based on each component's return, risk, and correlation with each other component. MPT demonstrates that if the components of a portfolio have low or negative mutual correlations, it may be possible to reduce risk without sacrificing return.

Negative correlation: *See* **correlation**.

Negative real interest rates: *See* **real interest rates**.

Nominal: In general, "nominal," such as a "nominal return on an investment," means not adjusted for inflation. "Real" reflects that adjustment. If your CD offers a 2 percent coupon but inflation is 3 percent, you've earned a +2 percent nominal return but a –1 percent real return.

Nominal interest rates: Rates quoted in the market, unadjusted for **inflation**. Nominal rates have two components: inflation (the change in the CPI) and the **real interest rate**.

Optimization: Choosing the combination of decision variables that produces the best outcome in light of constraints. Generally an optimum is achieved by maximizing or minimizing an objective function (measure of achievement of a goal). Portfolio optimization entails choosing the proportions of the portfolio devoted to each of a set of assets.

Options: Contracts that give the purchaser the right to buy or sell an asset (such as 100 shares of stock) at a specified price. "Call" options give the right to buy, and "put" options the right to sell. Someone might buy a call option if they believe the price of the stock will go higher than the strike price. Options have an expiration date, so if the stock does not rise above the strike price, the option will expire worthless (known as being "out of the money"), and the seller of the call will not be obliged to sell the shares (the shares will not be "called away"). A seller of a call option who owns the asset to be called is selling a "covered" call; if they do not own it, they've sold a "naked call." Covered options are far less risky than naked ones.

Portfolio: A collection of assets combined to achieve diversification.

Positive correlation: *See* **correlation**.

Rally: Temporary interruption in the downward movement of an asset class's prices. Rallies are the mirror image of **corrections**. It is not uncommon for **bull markets** to be punctuated by corrections and **bear markets** by rallies.

Real: Adjusted for inflation, by subtracting the inflation rate. *See* also **nominal**.

Real interest rates: Nominal interest rates adjusted for inflation (by subtracting it). If a certificate of deposit (CD) pays a 3 percent nominal rate, but inflation is 2 percent, investors receive only 1 percent of added purchasing power through interest payments. In other words, the CD's *real* interest rate is 1 percent. Real interest rates can be negative: if the same CD offers a nominal 3 percent and inflation is 5 percent, it pays a negative 2 percent real rate. Economists assess central bank monetary policy by computing real interest rates. Negative real rates are economically stimulative, while positive rates are restrictive. In 2009, the Fed kept short-term nominal rates near zero, while inflation was between 1 percent and 2 percent. So real rates were roughly negative 1 percent, a stimulative policy. Investors' great concern in late 2009 and early 2010 was that the Fed would stimulate for too long.

Rebalancing: The act of selling portfolio components whose current weight exceeds its asset allocation target, and using the funds to purchase assets whose weight is below its target. Implicitly the investor is "selling high" and "buying low" without any specific timing or foreknowledge. Rebalancing has been found to modest increase long-term returns, mainly by selling overbought assets before they fall and buying oversold assets before they rise. Generally, rebalancing should be an occasional process, either scheduled (say, annually) or whenever asset weights fall outside of bands around their targets.

Return on investment (ROI): The excess an investor receives over the amount he invested. In general, higher-risk investments must offer higher average returns to attract investment. In an efficient market, each investment's risk-adjusted return should be about the same.

Risk-adjusted return: An investment's return, adjusting for variability in that return, typically by dividing by its standard deviation. The Sharpe ratio (named after Nobelist William Sharpe) makes this computation.

Rule of 72: A simple rule of thumb that provides an approximation of the effects of compounding sufficient to double the value of an asset: If you know its average growth rate in percent, divide that number (omitting the percent sign) into the number 72 to get the number of periods needed for the asset to double in value. For example, an asset that grows at 6 percent per year will require 12 years (72 divided by 6) to double. At 8 percent per year, it will need 9 years (72 divided by 8) to double. The Rule of 72 is not exact but is a reasonable approximation of the complicated math of compounding. It is also useful for increases of more than a factor of 2. For example, a factor of 8 increase is 2 to the third power, so the Rule of 72 could be applied 3 times over.

Savings: The portion of an individual's income that is not consumed. Savings are the source of all **investment**, so a nation with a low savings rate must either borrow from other sources or reduce investment.

Short selling: Borrowing and selling an asset in anticipation that its price will drop so that you can buy it back at the new lower price to meet your obligation to your lender. Short selling of bonds by those concerned about a nation's fiscal policy can put great pressure on its bond prices or its currency. A technique often used by disgruntled **bond vigilantes**.

Sovereign wealth funds: Investment funds maintained by the governments of countries that run budget **surpluses**, usually because the nation exports more than it imports (e.g., oil-exporting countries). These funds act much like other institutional investors, except that their client is, directly or indirectly, a national government. This leads to concerns that these funds' capital will be deployed in pursuit of foreign policy goals, not commercial goals.

Spread: The difference between interest rates of two different fixed income instruments (e.g., corporate vs. treasury bonds). Used as an indicator of how investors view the comparative riskiness of the two instruments. In late 2008, spreads between most other types of bonds and treasuries widened greatly, as investors who were spooked by market turmoil rushed to the safety of treasuries, bidding down their yields and bidding up the yields of other issues. (Remember that bond yields vary inversely with bond prices.) *See* also **yield curve**.

Standard deviation: A measure of an asset price's **volatility**. Computed as the square root of each time period's squared deviations from the mean price for all periods. *See* also **variance**.

Sterilization: When a central bank prevents its increase in the money supply from depreciating the value of the currency. Commonly this is done by simultaneously issuing currency and bonds, in the expectation that investors will buy the bonds and thereby take currency out of circulation.

Stocks: Claims on a portion of the assets of a company. Also known as **equities**, because common stock owners own a portion of the company's equity: its net worth. **Preferred stockholders** also own a share of company equity, but they take precedence over common stockholders if the company is liquidated (i.e., its assets are sold off).

Total return: The sum of an investor's returns stemming from **dividends** received, plus gains in the price of the asset (**capital gains**). Over the past 80 or more years, the total return of stocks has averaged in the high single digits in percent. But in the decade of the 2000s, stocks' total return was close to zero, because the decade was bookended by bear markets.

Variance: The sum of an asset price's deviation each time period, squared, from the mean for all time periods. The square root of variance is **standard deviation.**

Volatility: Variation in the price of an asset or in its growth rate. Investors, of course, are happy with volatility on the upside but less so with downside volatility. For stocks, the most common measure of volatility is **beta**.

Yield curve: The profile of interest rates offered by bonds of different maturities. Generally, investors demand higher yields to lend their money for longer periods, so the yield curve is upward sloping. An inversion of the yield curve—where short-maturity bonds offer higher yields than long maturities—has been an excellent predictor of recession, because it implies that investors expect rates to fall in the future. This usually happens when demand for capital dries up because firms see declining sales and no longer wish to make investments in adding productive capacity.

Summary

Quantitative trading strategies have come to dominate the world's major capital markets. At their core, most of these strategies entail identifying mispriced assets using computer algorithms. The strategies are used in a wide range of applications: From augmenting traditional portfolio management, to exploiting arbitrage opportunities using computers colocated at the exchanges very rapidly and in high volume. While quant strategies have made a number of its leaders into multibillionaires, they have also greatly magnified markets' inherent volatility—from Black Monday of October 19, 1987, to the Flash Crash of May 6, 2010, each was traced back to programmed or high-frequency trading.

Several good journalistic accounts of quants have been published, including *The Quants* by Scott Patterson (2010), *The Big Short* (2010) by Michael Lewis, *More Money than God: Hedge Funds and the Making of the New Elite* by Sebastian Mallaby (2010), and *When Genius Failed: The Rise and Fall of Long-Term Capital Management* (2000) by Roger Lowenstein. While these offer interesting character studies and valuable cautionary tales, none dives very deeply into how quantitative strategies work. Many readers seek such tools so that they can improve on current practice—from the inside, at hedge funds, or from the outside, as regulators or advocates.

This book will be of interest to a variety of readers, including:

- Finance students who need an introduction to the IT underlying trading systems
- Investing students who wish to understand how quant strategies can affect their portfolios
- Individual investors considering investing in "quant" mutual funds and ETFs, which are increasing prevalent as Wall Street markets "absolute return" products
- Public policy students interested in asset market regulation
- Journalism students who wish to understand the markets they cover

Index

OTHER TITLES FROM THE ECONOMICS COLLECTION

Philip Romero, The University of Oregon and Jeffrey Edwards,
North Carolina A&T State University, Editors

- *Your Macroeconomic Edge: Investing Strategies for the Post-Recession World* by Philip J. Romero
- *Working with Economic Indicators: Interpretation and Sources* by Donald Stengel
- *Innovative Pricing Strategies to Increase Profits* by Daniel Marburger
- *Regression for Economics* by Shahdad Naghshpour
- *Statistics for Economics* by Shahdad Naghshpour
- *How Strong Is Your Firm's Competitive Advantage?* by Daniel Marburger
- *A Primer on Microeconomics* by Thomas Beveridge
- *Game Theory: Anticipating Reactions for Winning Actions* by Mark L. Burkey
- *A Primer on Macroeconomics* by Thomas Beveridge
- *Economic Decision Making Using Cost Data: A Guide for Managers* by Daniel Marburger
- *The Fundamentals of Money and Financial Systems* by Shahdad Naghshpour
- *International Economics: Understanding the Forces of Globalization for Managers* by Paul Torelli
- *The Economics of Crime* by Zagros Madjd-Sadjadi
- *Money and Banking: An Intermediate Market-Based Approach* by William D. Gerdes
- *Basel III Liquidity Regulation and Its Implications* by Mark A. Petersen and Janine Mukuddem-Petersen
- *Saving American Manufacturing: The Fight for Jobs, Opportunity, and National Security* by William R. Killingsworth
- *Advanced Economies and Emerging Markets: Prospects for Globalization* by Marcus Goncalves, José Alves, Carlos Frota, Harry Xia and Rajabahadur V. Arcot

Announcing the Business Expert Press Digital Library

*Concise E-books Business Students Need
for Classroom and Research*

This book can also be purchased in an e-book collection by your library as
- a one-time purchase,
- that is owned forever,
- allows for simultaneous readers,
- has no restrictions on printing, and
- can be downloaded as PDFs from within the library community.

Our digital library collections are a great solution to beat the rising cost of textbooks. E-books can be loaded into their course management systems or onto students' e-book readers.

The **Business Expert Press** digital libraries are very affordable, with no obligation to buy in future years. For more information, please visit **www.businessexpertpress.com/librarians**. To set up a trial in the United States, please email **sales@businessexpertpress.com**.

www.ingramcontent.com/pod-product-compliance
Lightning Source LLC
Chambersburg PA
CBHW050502190326
41458CB00005B/1397